Tales of the Sabine Borderlands

NUMBER SEVENTY-NINE:
The Centennial Series
of the Association of Former Students,
Texas A&M University

Tales of the Sabine Borderlands

Early Louisiana and Texas Fiction
by Théodore Pavie

Edited with an Introduction and Notes by Betje Black Klier

Translations by Betje Black Klier, Anne C. Marsh,
Philip Stewart, and Alexandra K. Wettlaufer

Texas A&M University Press
COLLEGE STATION

The paper used in this book meets the minimum requirements
of the American National Standard for Permanence
of Paper for Printed Library Materials, z39.48-1984.
Binding materials have been chosen for durability.

Library of Congress Cataloging-in-Publication Data

Pavie, Théodore.
    Tales of the Sabine borderlands : early Louisiana
and Texas fiction / by Théodore Pavie ; edited with an
introduction and notes by Betje Black Klier ;
translations by Betje Black Klier ... [et al .] . — 1st ed.
        p.   cm. — (Centennial series of the Association
of Former Students, Texas A&M University ; no. 79)
    Includes bibliographical references (p.).
    Contents : The myth of Sabine — Introduction —
1. Le nègre / translated by Philip Stewart — 2. Le
lazo / translated by Betje Black Klier — 3. La peau
d'ours / translated by Betje Black Klier and Anne C.
Marsh — 4. El cachupin / translated by Alexandra K.
Wettlaufer — Notes.
        ISBN 0-89096-837-3 (cloth : alk. paper). — ISBN
0-89096-854-3 (paper : alk. paper)
        1. Louisiana—History—Fiction.   2. Texas—History—
Fiction.   3. Sabine River Region (Tex. and La.)—
History—Fiction.   I. Klier, Betje Black.
II. Title. III. Series.
PQ2380.P44T35   1998
843´ .7—dc21   98-22081
                                                        CIP

CONTENTS

ILLUSTRATIONS

ACKNOWLEDGMENTS

I would like to thank a number of people with whom I have shared my enthusiasm for Théodore Pavie and who, in turn, helped bring this project to fruition. Yves Pavie helped me locate copies of two of the stories, and Charles Cronin, Charlie Junkerman, Diane North, and Josine Smits made numerous helpful suggestions. For editorial assistance in English, I am indebted to Patience Young and Mary Ellen Foley, and to Michèle Shockey and Myrna Rochester in French, in addition to my co-translators, Anne Marsh, Philip Stewart, and Alexandra Wettlaufer. Gen Guzman, Corrine Pluska, and Anne Marsh contributed to the inventory of Pavie's flora and fauna, which biologist Wm. D. (Bill) Reese cheerfully and copiously interpreted.

Electronic help came from Texas and Louisiana. Ron Tyler, Carl Brasseaux, and Mary Len Wernet helped make it possible for me to write a book about the Sabine Borderlands while living in California and working in the incomparable libraries of Stanford University, whose congenial staff I also sincerely thank.

Chuck and Anne Phillips welcomed me in Nacogdoches, and Conna Cloutier and daughter Marcie, the most gracious hostesses in Natchitoches, stayed at-the-ready with encouraging words and delicious Creole coffee as did Erbon and Marie Wise in Sulphur, Louisiana. Pascale Voisin cheerfully filled my cup in Paris, as did other descendants of Théodore Pavie's brother, Victor: Cathérine, Gilles and Odette, and Serge and Pierrette. Gabrielle and Yves graciously received me in the South of France where Yves and I became the armchair travelers for whom Uncle Théodore wrote these stories. For your assistance, enthusiasm, and hospitality, thank you.

In addition to years of encouragement and practical support, Paul Klier provided the technical assistance to bring all of these contributions together into a volume which we hope brings the voice of Théodore Pavie back for the twenty-first century to tell tales of the Sabine Borderlands— this time in English.

THE MYTH OF SABINE

Today, in the two small college towns of Nacogdoches, Texas, and Natchitoches, Louisiana, more or less equidistant from the Sabine River, you may hear the story told of the wise old chief of the Nachidoche Indians, who loved his two sons equally. Rather than leave his lands to one or the other, or lose one or both of his sons in a contest of might, he persuaded them to meet at the river. There, he instructed each son to rise on the morrow and run until the sun set, one toward the east and one toward the west. The young men were to start new tribes, and each would be given the land he covered with his legs in one course of the sun. Their new tribes spanned the distance between Natchitoches and Nacogdoches.

There, in the Sabine Borderlands, the Spanish who were moving northward through Mexico and the French who were pushing southward from Canada met, overlapped, clashed, traded, and eventually fused in the space along the Sabine River, which divides Louisiana and Texas today. As if influenced by recurring manifestations of the historic subconscious of the land, the area has been forever blessed and cursed with the pride and rivalry of the brothers, who may have been somewhat less wise than their father Sabine, whose kingdom they divided.

INTRODUCTION

The myth of Sabine mediates the visible and the merely plausible, what can be seen and what can be imagined. Its folkloric style enhances the believability of the story, as does the existence of the two towns whose names confound visitors today: Nacogdoches and Natchitoches. Tense pairs embody a rivalry—East and West, North and South, France and Spain, Canada and Mexico—the essence of brothers, tribes, and empires.

Just as the rivalry between the native Hainais and Kadohadacho tribes separated them before the arrival of the Europeans, the Spanish and French played out their colonial rivalry along the Sabine River between Nacogdoches and Natchitoches. Napoleon intervened briefly to keep the English out of the contest. Mexico and the United States emerged as the next contenders for the land where freedom bordered slavery, under the eyes and guns of settlers and bandits.

While I was gathering material for this book, I always called the project "Nac-to-Nac," pronounced like "back-to-back," because I found it amusing that local residents on both sides of the Sabine call their towns "Nac," despite the spelling of the first syllable. Moreover, Natchitoches (Nak-ə-tish) has three syllables, and Nacogdoches (Nak-ə-dō-chəs) has four. The fates of the two "Nacs" —the old Spanish presidio, Nacogdoches, and the former French outpost, Natchitoches—were intertwined long before 1803 when Thomas Jefferson's diplomats purchased "Louisiana" from Napoléon Bonaparte without designating the borders.

By 1805, Jefferson realized that his diplomats had reached a stalemate with Spain in settling the western boundary of its purchase and establishing the border between the United States and Mexico. In October, 1806, armed Mexican and American troops faced each other across the Sabine River. War seemed imminent. To avoid conflict and buy time, Jefferson directed Madison to inform the U.S. emissary to make a provisional agreement to retain the status quo. Mexico could keep its military presence in Nacogdoches and the United States could maintain its presence in Natchitoches. Both countries could increase their troops, provided neither patrolled the interim space or tolerated the establishment of new settlements between them.[1] Before Jefferson's instructions reached Louisiana, his emissary, Gen. James Wilkinson, reached a similar accord with Gen. Simón de Herrera, the commander of the Mexican troops. Exchanging only letters, Wilkinson and Herrera created the Neutral Ground east of the Sabine. Their agreement, never formalized as a treaty, lasted from 1806 to 1819, when it was superseded by the Adams-Onís Treaty between the United States and Spain, two years prior to Mexican independence.[2] While law enforcement was suspended, brigands and pirates and thieves arrived. Many suspected the loyalty of Wilkinson, Jefferson's highest-ranking military officer. Documents now prove that he was a double agent in the service of Spain when he concluded the Neutral Ground agreement.[3] But is it treason to do the right thing for the wrong reason?

Before Americans could traverse the land in numbers great enough to separate Texas from Coahuila and Mexico, then "remove" the majority of Native Americans from their homeland, a moment of international stasis was reached. This book carries the reader to that era of tense calm when Théodore Pavie roamed the borderland trails, captured its images, and sensed the underlying strife.

THÉODORE PAVIE

In 1829 Théodore Pavie left his job in his father's publishing house in Angers, in the Loire Valley in France, to spend the winter in Louisiana on his uncle's plantation on the Red River. Charles Pavie, a veteran of the early Napoleonic campaigns, had been settled for some twenty-five years in Natchitoches where he married a Creole of Canadian and French descent.[4] Shortly after his arrival in Louisiana, eighteen-year-old Théodore accompanied Charles and his Creole brother-in-law on a westward trek from Natchitoches, which was still primarily French, through the former Neutral Ground and across the Sabine River to Nacogdoches, Texas, which remained under Mexican rule.

In Nacogdoches they stayed with John Durst[5] in the two-story stone building known as the Old Stone Fort. The Pavie men met Colonel José de las Piedras, commander of the military outpost. They also encountered a tribe of Comanche Indians and attended a horse race held two miles from the presidio. These events occurred during a brief respite in the power struggle among colonists, officials in Mexican Texas, and Anglo-American filibusters lurking in Louisiana.

As it happened, Pavie visited Nacogdoches just two months before the Mexican congress passed the infamous Law of April 6, 1830. This law, passed while Pavie was visiting New Orleans and just before he returned to France, would have limited future immigration to Texas from the United States and sent Mexican convicts to Texas to serve their terms as soldiers. Instead, the law triggered the final series of rebellions that led to the Texas Revolution, which permanently separated the region from Mexico. Pavie recorded the events of his journey in *Souvenirs atlantiques,* which he completed after he returned to Angers.[6] His father published twenty copies of the book in Angers in 1832 as thank-you gifts for his son's hosts.

The following year, the Roret publishing house in Paris produced a slightly expanded, two-volume edition of *Souvenirs atlantiques* for the public. Two of the three chapters appended to that edition were set in the Louisiana-Texas Borderlands.

The Texas story added to that edition, "Le Lazo" ("The Lasso"), marks the beginning of Borderlands literature.[7] "Le Lazo" is the first published fiction set in Texas and written by an eyewitness in a literary form with no other intention than to entertain. Pavie's tale, which villainizes Piedras, was published three years prior to the Texas Revolution, when Texas and the rest of the United States radically revised their opinion of Santa Anna—the Mexican arch-villain whom Piedras refused to support.

"Le Lazo" also introduces a panoply of details that later became important themes in Western literature: romance, rodeos, horses, soldiers, intuitive Native Americans, poor widowed fathers devoted to beautiful daughters who peek from behind mantillas. *Le Far West* begins here! Pavie's tale predates the split of Texas letters into Mexican and Western streams and introduces a Tejano hero into Mexican Texas literature (1819–36).[8] The young French author unites horseman, Mexican, and European brigand in a single character named Antonio, who is devoted to his señorita and, Prometheus-like, fights for justice against colonial authority.[9]

The Louisiana story that Pavie added to the Roret edition of *Souvenirs atlantiques,* "Le Nègre," is an ethnographic treasure. Notable for its descriptions of slaves in a separate, nocturnal society of their own creation,[10] the story serves as a prototype abolitionist text. In "Le Nègre," a "noble slave" replaces the noble savage dear to Pavie's generation. His protagonist is reminiscent of the rebellious slave in *Bug Jargal,* Victor Hugo's novel set in Saint-Domingue (today's Haiti). Once a tribal king in Africa, Hugo's character led his people into armed rebellion, but Pavie's character eschews violence in favor of rhetoric. He speaks for his people in a voice calculated to move the reader to despise the institution of slavery. Instead of abstract moral argument, "Le Nègre" presents two characters—one black, one white—suffering the degrading consequences of enslavement. The story provokes a sympathetic response for the black slave and feelings of antipathy toward the white overseer. Reworking a story from Angers about a soldier hiding in a log during the Vendéan counterrevolution (the local Catholic uprising against the French Revolution), Pavie made significant additions based on his experiences in Louisiana where he stayed in a cottage from which he observed slaves singing and dancing around the evening fire to the accompaniment of gourd banjos.[11]

Théodore Pavie continued to travel, study, and make notes and sketches for another decade. He became a linguist and recorded the world's cultures as they evolved—and sometimes vanished—between 1830 and 1865. Although most of his work during this long period involved scholarly translations such as *The Life of Krishna* or the Indian epic, *The Mahabharata,* he also wrote two new stories set in Louisiana and Texas, where the cultures he had observed in 1829–30 were also rapidly changing or even disappearing.

Pavie, too, was changing, as were the products of his pen. Long paragraphs appear, a feature we have retained in this volume where punctuation has been modernized. His aptitude for describing the material and natural world never wavered. Violence continued to play a significant role in his plots while the social and cultural components grew richer. Whereas the first two stories in this collection are the efforts of a talented schoolboy who anticipated returning to his father's print shop to publish his older brother's poems, his later work shows the influence of prominent writers and scholars such as Sainte-Beuve, Eugène Bournouf, and Buloz, who took an active interest in his literary output.[12]

During fifteen years of traveling and thirty years of writing for the *Revue des Deux Mondes,* France's most significant literary periodical in the nineteenth century, Pavie became a popular reporter and interpreter of exotic cultures. France's armchair travelers were enthralled by his observations embodied in fictional characters situated in richly depicted contexts. Pavie, like many writers of his generation, began his career imitating the melancholic Chateaubriand,[13] but today he might be called the "Balzac of the Borderlands"[14] because of his seamless blending of observation and invention. Although many of the characters in their stories are fictional, Honoré de Balzac and Pavie created settings and plots full of historical detail and cultural truths. Yet the well-traveled, multilingual, financially independent Pavie was far more modern and inclusive than Balzac, the Paris-centric, monolingual, financially strapped genius whom he outlived by a quarter of a century.

Influenced throughout his life by the German philosopher Friedrich von Schiller, Pavie sought the Romantic ideal propounded by Schiller of a unity that includes all diversity. Pavie's collected stories present a picture of the culture between Nacogdoches and Natchitoches that has unity despite the tensions of its rich diversity. While many told the Anglo-American story of the purchase of Louisiana and the conquest of Texas, Pavie alone wove his plots around the other players in the story. His style allows readers to grasp cultural differences at the origin of conflicts. He uses a painterly eye to describe settings and an ethnographic gaze to fix cultures, seamlessly interlacing descriptions of nature with perceptive human observations. Prompted by his travel notes and sketchbooks, he continued to generate stories from his travels until 1865 when he left Paris and returned to Angers.

Pavie's third and fourth stories of the Sabine Borderlands, "La Peau d'ours" ("The Bearskin") and "El Cachupin," were published in the *Revue des Deux Mondes* in 1850 and 1861 respectively. "Gachupín" was the name North Americans gave to European-born Spaniards, who were banished from Mexico after its independence in 1821.[15] Both tales were probably written to satisfy a demand for stories of the Borderlands.[16] The Mexican War (1846–48) had reawakened French interest in the region at the time of the publication of "La Peau d'ours." Similarly, the issues leading to the unfortunate French intervention in Mexico (1862–67) must have stimulated interest in the 1861 publication of "El Cachupin."

These stories later found their way into an anthology of distended short stories or novellas to be read at a single sitting. "La Peau d'ours" reappears in his collection of tales from overseas for armchair travelers titled *Scènes et Récits des pays d'outremer.*[17] Pavie may have been influenced by his contemporary, Edgar Allen Poe, to infuse a tale with irrational fear. (Poe's works, skillfully translated by poet-journalist Charles Baudelaire, would have received renewed attention in France after his death in 1849). Seeking a plausible historic cause for life-threatening fear, so out of phase with the story's bucolic setting, Pavie turned to a little known incident in which Comanches from West Texas terrified white settlers in East Texas and across the Sabine as far as Natchitoches. Pavie's French readers would have found both the setting—Natchitoches and the Neutral Ground—and the main characters—Canadian traders—exotic. The plot, which evolves from a culturally insensitive gesture—a public shove—and its fatal consequences, resembles another story in the *Scènes et Récits* collection, "Les Babouches du Brahmane," set in India.[18] But Pavie transcended the incident, casting the rapidity of change in modern life as the villain. Within the backlash of cultural changes too rapid to absorb, a displaced Native American is set on a collision course with an economically displaced Canadian family. In his introduction, Pavie laments, "De nos jours, tout change, et trop vite sous le soleil!" ("In our times, everything under the sun changes too rapidly!")

Time caught up with the traveler. Pavie died in 1896, three years before the fourth tale, "El Cachupin," resurfaced in America.[19] One of the story's subplots, the fate of doña Jacinta's father and his ship, bears an uncanny resemblance to a strand in the legend of the pirate Jean Laffite, whose evil lieutenant plundered an American ship against Laffite's wishes. Pavie may have learned this story either from his uncle or from one of Laffite's former contacts, who included John Durst.

As a world traveler and expert in the epic stories of numerous cultures, Pavie developed a dramatic style that advances the plot through cross-cultural intersections. Trapped in these intersections, his characters demonstrate their lack of cross-cultural understanding and struggle with the consequences. The tales from Texas and Louisiana provide vivid examples of Pavie's special talent for storytelling, his gift for powerfully depicting milieu, and weaving social fabric. He builds a "culturescape," peopled with characters with evocative names, which preserves for the reader the vanished riches of 1830 in the Sabine Borderlands.

After Pavie's death in 1896, his works slipped into quiet oblivion until the regions about which he wrote gained enough cultural maturity to rediscover them. The four stories in this volume bring new light to the diversity of the land from Nacogdoches to Natchitoches. Remarkable early examples of American ethnographic fiction, they are treasure-troves of historical detail.

Tales of the Sabine Borderlands

Le Nègre

EDITOR'S NOTES

"Le Nègre" is set in an identifiable region but lacks the identifiable historical events of the other three stories in this collection. The precise moment of the action cannot be fixed. The story takes place during an era when African slaves worked the plantations, yet this was true throughout the span of white settlement in Louisiana and Texas before Pavie's visit in 1829. The river mentioned is the Washita, or Ouachita, which Native Americans called the Black River. This would anchor the story to Louisiana, probably near a former Spanish enclave called Fort Miró.

GROUPS REPRESENTED
BY THE CHARACTERS

Unlike other white observers, Pavie described the internal dynamics of the slave community, noting nuances of racial blend, generational differences, and political status. The tragic hero had been a tribal chief in Africa before tacitly assuming leadership among his people in America. Pavie contrasts his nobility with the inhumanity of the white community, personified by the overseer. Pavie conveys the unity of a slave community in this elemental tale of good and evil.

BIOGRAPHICAL ELEMENTS

Three years before leaving for America, fourteen-year-old Théodore Pavie became friends with Victor Hugo, who was already much admired for his literary prowess. Although Hugo never visited the New World, he had already penned his first novel, *Bug Jargal,* in which the rebel leader of the slave uprisings in Saint-Domingue had once been a king in Africa.[1] In subsequent works, Pavie's characters are rooted in his experience of Borderland life. Witness, for example, his naming a character "Mercury" (in a story with a "Kate," "Dick," and "Bill"), the name of one of Charles Pavie's elderly slaves. But in this early story, Pavie seems to have drawn his inspiration from literature instead of life. His character is patterned after Hugo's exotic literary hero and presented in a setting embellished with precise details of local color: possums, swamp mosquitoes ("marin gouins"), gourd banjos ("banjas") and a copper milk pail for a drum.

Pavie had a strong music background. He sang and played the flute, and he had an excellent grasp of canonical and contemporary music. His exceptional musicological knowledge allowed him to describe primitive African instruments previously ignored or slighted by European visitors. His description of a slave dance is remarkable not only for the sense of motion it conveys, but also for the absence of the condescension so common among whites in the region. Rather than preach abolition, Pavie conveys the humiliation inherent in the institution of slavery.

We may infer from the style and content of this story that Pavie wrote "Le Nègre" after observing nocturnal plantation life, yet before his trip to Texas in February, 1830. His writing bears traces of neo-classicism drawn from his education, merged with the Romantic effusion of his idols, Chateaubriand and Hugo. Following his journey to Nacogdoches, the young author shed such ponderous noble language as "the queen of the night's dazzling disk," in favor of more direct vocabulary. While dramatic moons continued to be a feature of his landscapes, they were updated and localized as "harvest moons" or "Comanche moons." It was after writing "Le Nègre" and visiting Texas that Pavie demonstrates that he understood that he was participating in history by living in a vivid moment that would not return. He began to frame his stories within a specific historical moment, localized to time and place by echoes of identifiable events and intricate descriptions.

LIBERTY, LIBERTY OR DEATH!

Moonlight gilded the banks of the Washita; the air was still burning hot. Mosquitoes, coming out of the marshes, darted among the cane with a high-pitched hum; the queen of the night's dazzling disk appeared as a globe of fire through a prism of vapors; herds, fleeing the woods where they are devoured by insects, came to bleat and bellow at lake's edge; and roes, provoked by bites from swamp mosquitoes,[2] sent a plaintive moan echoing through the woods; the serpent slithered across humid trails in search of the worm-eaten roots that furnished him a retreat; turtles were digging in the sand to lay their eggs; and the rattle of the crocodile, asleep on trees and vines ferried toward the sea by the current, rose like a sinister sigh from the deep, dark bed of the Black River.

In the tall grass along the bank a laughing band of Negroes was walking, armed with knotty, ironclad cudgels. They were followed by large panting dogs, their ears hanging, their tails lowered. A few of these blacks carried on their shoulders the fresh carcass of a wildcat or possum; others carefully cradled their red woolen hats, full of turtle eggs or wild fruit, while the children—negro, griffe,[3] or mulatto—knocked flowers off the bushes with their spears as they went past, bounding with the agility of fawns over the sinewy roots winding through the forest. When the group had reached the gate to the cabins, the overseer's harsh voice rose over their chants and was followed by a heavy silence. He threatened to whip and pillory anyone who returned late to camp, and every slave scurried to a place near him to establish his presence. The master's searching eyes surveyed this circle with inner satisfaction, and, content with his flock, he went and sat down nearby.

Then the slaves gathered in the middle of the camp. A large fire crackled in the center of the assembly, and that inborn instinct in all men who are still close to the state of nature, that causes them to find in the embers of the campfire, even during the burning nights of Louisiana, a consoling companion, brought them all in close to the flames, which rose in a spiral in the middle of a flat, elevated spot and were reflected against the dark green of the forests. Whatever the fatigue of the evening, the Negroes are always to be found thus gathered during the night, stirring the branches burning in the fire, chatting quietly with solemn gravity, and in this way leading a second, nocturnal life entirely their own. Daytime is devoted to the master's service.

When all was ready for the dance, one of the slaves tuned a crude guitar, cobbled from a gourd with bobcat gut, and began a prelude as with a Moorish mandolin. Another Negro turned over a copper vat used for milking the cows and beat out a prolonged roll that faded into the woods. Soon, at a signal from the guitarist, the dance began. Now there

This rare sketch of slave quarters preserves a view of Louisiana that few visitors recorded. Pavie was interested in all aspects of Louisiana life and in capturing minute details such as the boats to bring cotton from the opposite shore of the river. *Sketch by Théodore Pavie, 1829–30. Courtesy Chasle Pavie Collection*

would be rapid stamping, the dancers clapping their thighs and hands to the rhythm, spinning about, or suddenly stopping with an expression of surprise and pleasure; now they would all join in a round, with groups smartly splitting off; and the Creole round described a vast circle about the campfire. The songs varied with the musicians' inspiration. Sometimes there were the melancholic chants to which slaves from Africa evoke their lost freedom; and when the young Negresses repeated them, there came from the circle of ancients a monotone, sustained murmur that rose to the highest notes to accompany that sad and plaintive melody from another hemisphere.

"Dance me the dance of the Congos!" said the overseer then, approaching the group of slaves when they were taking a moment's rest, and they obeyed as if it were an order. Three old Negroes tuned their banjos, and three others took over marking the beat and drumroll. The almost military movements of this African dance recombined in all directions, and rhythmic fingers snapped over the Negroes' kinky heads. Attention was at its peak. Hunched in a circle, these black men, half-naked, their heads resting on their arms and their arms on their knees, looked like demons overtaken by daylight in their nocturnal frolics. Their large eyes remained motionless; their wide, open mouths revealed a row of white teeth between which their breath glided soundlessly and mixed with smoke. The flame played in greenish reflections over all those black, satanic bodies. The overseer himself, with the pale and livid hue of a white man tanned by the sun, was watching the dance of all these brutish creatures, which he set in motion with a single gesture of his whip, when a colossal form appeared above the barrier and something heavy rolled in toward the flames.

A cry of surprise arose from the assembly. The overseer reflexively had snatched up his whip. "Late again!" he cried furiously, addressing the gigantic Negro who had just bounded into the midst of his own. "Down, dog!" And the whip cracked like a sinister bark in the forest. A stripe of blood ran down the haunches of the slave, who rolled on the ground screaming with rage and biting the grass, whitened with his foam.

"Master," he stammered, "look what I was bringing you. This damned roe led me far afield, but there it is. It's for you. Forgive me, forgive me, master!"

Kicking away the broad hands clasping his knees, the overseer replied with a second whiplash, and the bloodied leather knots struck the exposed bones and resounded dully.

The other Negroes had withdrawn. He whom they venerated like a chief and whose absence they had vainly striven to conceal from their master's wrath lay motionless. The white man looked at him with wild eyes inflamed with fury, and nothing could be heard but a stifled rattle that still swelled the rebel slave's bloodied chest. There was a minute's silence during which the Negro struggled against pain, fear, and hatred. Then all at once he pulled himself up, and the immense shadow projected by his huge frame seemed to swallow up the planter's frail, slight image in the shades of death. "Master," he said, grasping in one fist his enemy's two arms, "I loved you. I have saved your life when the Indians pillaged your house and possessions, I have fought day and night the floodwaters that threatened your harvest, I have seeded your fields for thirty years. You have yoked me like an ox to the plow, and I have dug my furrow, I who was free and great in my tribe of black men. It was I who saddled your horse, who knelt to hold your stirrup, it was I who slept across your threshold! . . . That's enough said. Oh! you tremble, you can't cry out. Have no fear. I was chief of a tribe. I scorn you, but I do not take vengeance. But you shall never see me again, you shall never again have me following you like a shadow. I will mock your wrath. And from the midst of this flock of men who tremble under your words, this head, the one held highest, will never again bow before you!"

The master, left to the mercy of his offended slave, had not the strength to reply. The Negro took off a yucca belt that carried his cutlass and with it bound his opponent's two arms tightly; then, taking him in his arms like a child, he said in his ear, "Farewell, you who said you were my master. I no longer know any master on this earth." And he leapt over the barrier.

The powerful Negro hurled himself into the river. He swam with one arm and held his cutlass aloft with the other to fend off the crocodiles he saw breathing at the water's surface. On the opposite bank, he grabbed a grazing wild horse by the mane, and, throwing a rope around its neck, he clung to its back with the suppleness of a reptile. Seated sidewise on the mighty beast, which he spurred on with the point of his dagger, he disappeared like a centaur into the brush. Sparks flew from the panting horse's four hooves; it seemed to fly, and its flowing black mane swept the dust. Thus the Negro fled, unmindful that death was following him step for step and that his first halt would be a tomb. He galloped on, reciting the song of his tribe; his sonorous voice rose through the silence of the night to the tops of the cypress trees, and when he stopped now and then, he listened in fascination as the echoes repeated whole refrains.

The fugitive slave sang and the air whistled through his thick hair. At daybreak, the horse collapsed; chance had cast them near an old settlement the horseman recognized. For a long time he roamed alone on foot; and making out a trail now covered over, he went to take refuge during the day amid the sugarcane.

Meanwhile the master had pulled himself up, and his imperious voice had forced the Negroes out of their hut. He went to get the dogs, and from the place where the unfortunate had grabbed onto the horse, his trail was constantly followed. At length his companions in slavery trudged glum and silent to the edge of the field that served as the Negro's retreat. There, the overseer ordered them, under pain of death, to encircle the cane; the dogs were unleashed on the beaten road, and the master advanced with ax in hand. Through the smooth, green shoots of the recent planting, all at once they saw the rebel's gigantic frame stand fearfully erect. At the sight of his former master, the Negro clapped his bleeding hands over his head and uttered a loud cry. The only reply was the crack of the overseer's rifle, and one of the fugitive's two arms was no longer up in the air. Then he hid in the sugarcane, and whether his comrades facilitated his escape, or he evaded their vigilance, he disappeared.

The following winter the same Negroes, under the same overseer, were clearing broad areas in the inner forest. One enormous tree long resisted the flame; its flowing sap prevented it from burning. The Negroes were obliged to saw through its roots; it fell with a tremendous thud and split wide open. What was the workers' surprise when they saw a long, whitened skeleton come out of its trunk and break to pieces with the fragments of the great tree! They looked at each other full of terror, and the master imposed silence on one of them who asserted that the skeleton had but one arm!

Le Lazo

EDITOR'S NOTES

Three circumstances of Mexican history fix the time line of this tale, an enigmatic blend of reportage and imagination. The first is an 1826 land title dispute in East Texas that erupted into an armed insurrection. Although this episode, known as the Fredonian Rebellion, was quickly controlled, it triggered a reinforcement of Mexican troops in Nacogdoches in 1827. Having no place to quarter the new troops, the commander seized the parish church and converted it into barracks for his men. The impoverished Mexican government had no money either to build barracks or aid in the construction of a new church.[1] Though no image has survived, Pavie calls the makeshift barracks a "hangar," from an old French word meaning a shed used for warehousing materials.

The commander of the reinforcements was Colonel José de las Piedras, a Creole from Santa Fé, a small harbor village on stilts near Veracruz. Unlike Pavie's fictionalized character in "Le Lazo," the real Piedras remained in this difficult command for five years until the Battle of Nacogdoches in August, 1832, when American settlers defeated the Mexican troops. The Anglos who captured Piedras (including John Durst, Pavie's host in 1830) offered him the option of remaining in Nacogdoches if he would join them in support of Antonio López de Santa Anna, a Federalist who claimed to espouse the provisions of the Constitution of 1824. Piedras knew Santa Anna better than the colonists, who did not recognize Mephistopheles in disguise or weigh the long-term consequences of dealing with him. A loyal Centralist, Piedras refused to consent. James Bowie happened to arrive in Nacogdoches the day after the battle and escorted the prisoner to a boat bound for Matamoros, Mexico.

After Piedras's troops withdrew, the absence of any Mexican military presence east of San Antonio permitted Anglos to organize the rebellion that overthrew the government and defeated the Mexican army under Santa Anna at San Jacinto. After the Texas Revolution, during a confrontation between Federalist and Centralist forces at Tampico, Mexico, Piedras was captured. Santa Anna personally issued the order to have him shot. He was executed in 1839.[2]

The second event that fixes this story in time is the Spanish invasion of Mexico, in which Pavie's protagonist, Antonio, was supposedly a participant. In August, 1829, Spanish royalists attempting to reconquer Mexico invaded Tampico. The Mexican campaign against the Spanish invaders along the Gulf of Mexico brought to prominence two generals known to Texas history, Santa Anna and Manuel de Mier y Terán. The campaign also precipitated the final expulsion from Mexico of Spaniards—the detested Gachupines whom Pavie calls Cachupines. The story suggests that a small number of regular soldiers from the campaign at Veracruz and Tampico made their way through San Antonio to the presidio at Nacogdoches.

The third historical event is the passage of the Law of April 6, 1830, which perpetuated the administrative junction of Texas to the neighboring state of Coahuila, halted U.S. immigration, and triggered the next phase of Anglo rebellion against Mexican authorities. This law was a direct result of the recommendations of Terán, who had visited Nacogdoches in 1828–29 as the leader of the boundary commission to Texas. Despite the increased number of troops under Piedras's command, Terán concluded that the high percentage of Anglo colonists entering Mexico was an imminent threat to Mexican sovereignty that needed to be severely curtailed. For Anglos in East Texas, one important aspect of this law was that it dashed their hopes for an autonomous Texas, a right many colonists believed they had previously been granted in the Constitution of 1824. Restrictions imposed on importing slaves from the United States would also limit their livelihoods and the value of their landholdings.

"Le Lazo" is also historically significant because it gives us an early glimpse of roping and riding wild horses as a form of public entertainment, a spectacle that was destined to become one of the strongest images of the American West. Early Nacogdoches historian George Crocket made note of a racetrack on the high ground between Ironosa (Arenosa) Creek and the Attoyac River, near the present town of Swift and beside a

Mexican settlement known as the Mountain. The track was laid out by Lucian y Barbo, grandson of town founder Antonio Gil y Barbo, and an early settler simply called "Ward." Crocket describes the scene: "Ward and the Y'Barbos laid out a racetrack which was in use long afterwards and was known as Steddam's racetrack. Samuel Steddam, on whose land it was located, ran races there before and after the Texas revolution, and John Yarborough, his jockey, then a mere boy, testified that it was a very old place even at that time."[3]

This may have even been the track Pavie visited. Horse racing was not uncommon east of the Sabine River at this time, probably due to the presence in Louisiana of U.S. troops who brought a taste for the sport along with their paychecks. West of the Sabine, as Pavie's story shows, the cultural seeds had been planted for the transformation of horse races into rodeos that test many of the skills American cowboys learned from Mexican ranch hands.

GROUPS REPRESENTED BY THE CHARACTERS

Antonio represents Pavie's romantic European perspective on the new Mexican emerging from a blend of indigenous Indians and their Spanish conquerors. His name is strong and melodious, without the aristocratic pretensions of inherited nobility (not *don* Antonio or Antonio *de* los Pinos). He is brave, vigorous, and strong, and he is in harmony with natural forces such as an unbroken horse. Antonio is recognizable by his dress, which has been adapted to the New World—oversized spurs, a long blue cloak draped over his shoulder, and an ample grey felt hat decorated with an eagle feather. He helped to throw off the yoke of the Spaniards at Veracruz, and he continues to serve his fledgling country's military endeavors. Yet Antonio will resist anyone who threatens his legitimate right of self-determination.

Pavie's character don Piedras, based upon Colonel José de las Piedras, represents the Creoles. At this time, when only persons of full European—French or Spanish—extraction born in the New World were called Creoles, Piedras retains markings of aristocracy. He is addressed as *don* Piedras and calls himself this. The expulsion of the Gachupines from Mexico elevates him to the ruling class. As such, he is courteous yet cunning and intrinsically evil. Removed from nature, he relies on underlings to enforce his power and deal with the elements. His uniform displays recognizable symbols of power, including braids, a brown coat, and a white sombrero with an elegant feather. Like Napoleon and Santa Anna, Piedras rides a white horse.

A mysterious Delaware Indian who moves silently and instinctively through the forest in the night represents the Native American tribes who have taken refuge in Texas. In the company of soldiers, this Delaware tribesman is relegated to the unpleasant downwind side of the campfire, suggesting that he, like his nation, has been shunted to the most undesirable space. But he also has the confidence of the commander, who seeks and follows his advice. In 1830, immigrant Indians, forced out of the United States into Mexico, probably believed Piedras was the key to permanent land titles in Texas. Evidence for this is found in the aged Cherokee chief Bowles's unsuccessful attempt to come to the commander's aid against the Anglo faction at the Battle of Nacogdoches.

A range of underlings, including faceless officers and priests who carry out the commander's orders, completes the communal structure at the presidio. Many of these characters exhibit a blend of Old and New World attributes. For example, the priest's rosary is decorated with skulls of ivory while the drum major's baton is a sugarcane staff, and a hammock and parrot add exotic touches to the Mexican household. Mexican civilians who survived the colonial era are represented by Clara's venerable father, who smokes in his doorway in a striped cloak. Rosary-clutching Clara remains devoted to her father while vowing her love to Antonio. She represents the vessel of a new era.

BIOGRAPHICAL ELEMENTS

On February 23, 1830, Pavie wrote his father in France that he had just returned from an eight-day trek to Texas, where he "saw the chief of the Cherokees with his lance decorated with enemy scalps."[4] This dates his journey to Nacogdoches to mid-February, 1830. At the end of April, three months after attending the horse race in Nacogdoches, Pavie accompanied his aunt, uncle, and cousin to New Orleans for several weeks before setting sail for Bordeaux. News of the Law of April 6, 1830, probably reached him there before he set sail. His uncle, a cotton broker and a Mason, would have learned the news as quickly as it reached New Orleans.

In his home in Angers after the July Revolution,[5] Pavie completed *Souvenirs atlantiques,* which his father published as a family edition in 1832. In the chapter titled "Nacogdoches," Pavie describes the town and a horse race he attended during his visit. Some time before the public edition of *Souvenirs atlantiques* was published in 1833, the young author appended "Le Lazo" to his travel journal. In this story, full of associations with Romanticism, we see Pavie's conception of heroism and glory, which was akin to the heroism of the "brigand literature" so popular with his generation. Though artists depicted brigands as modern characters, they belonged to the older outlaw tradition of Robin Hood or, more recently, *Ivanhoe* by Sir Walter Scott (whom Pavie had visited in London in April, 1828). Historian Hugh Honour describes this early nineteenth-century literature, in which the bandit is "a fugitive from injustice, rather than from justice, obliged to take to the hills and survive as best he can, preserving his code of honor . . . a type of Romantic hero, passionate and melancholy, rugged as the untamed landscape into which he was so skilled at disappearing."[6] Recounting his Texas experience the second time, Pavie casts his heroic Mexican cavalryman as a Romantic brigand.

In "Nacogdoches," which appears to be Pavie's objective account of the horse race, an American jockey—possibly John Yarborough—vies with a six-foot-tall Mexican corporal of admirable athletic form and prowess, presumably the inspiration for Antonio. Pavie's two accounts of the race are parallel, down to the cloud of dust that rose as the racers flew by. From there the fictional account diverges. The young French spectator describes his intense experience in *Souvenirs atlantiques:*[7] "The two antagonists started off on foot. At the signal of the colonel, the two racers plunged into the arena. Screams of the spectators rose no more quickly than the clouds of dust in which the racers seemed to fly. Near me there were Indians, mouths agape, who watched stupefied and repeated, as in *The Last of the Mohicans,* their guttural exclamation: 'Ugh! Ugh!'" Though the English horse led at first, the Mexican steed shot past and "carried the winner into the forest, his long legs responding to its furious movements with so much grace that general applause arose."[8]

Pavie's description suggests the furious energy captured by the images of one of his heroes, Théodore Géricault, in paintings of the races of the riderless Barbieri horses in Rome or in *Mazeppa.* He also describes the riders as springing onto the horses' backs like panthers, reminiscent of similar paintings by George Stubbs or of the panthers depicted by his brother's friend Eugène Delacroix.[9] In addition to being an accomplished horseman, Pavie was familiar with formal riding practices in England and France, and his association with artists permitted him to see first-hand much of the significant art of his time.

The author's shift in attitude toward Piedras between "Nacogdoches" and "Le Lazo" may reflect the Anglo community's change in attitude toward Piedras after the Law of April 6, 1830, when the Creole commander became the lightning rod for frustrated American desire for Texas land. In the first edition, Pavie described Piedras as a competent man who maintained a cordial atmosphere among his men: "The colonel is a Creole from Vera Cruz—trained, distinguished, and extremely cordial toward foreigners: each day he comes to sit on the gallery [porch] of the hotel and talk with the travelers for whom he gladly provides an escort when it is a question of crossing Texas by the interior route. The cavalry-men who saw us chatting familiarly with him never hesitated to take off their hats in front of us, and on every occasion I had to be impressed with their extreme courtesy." Note, however, that he does not use the colonel's name. In "Le Lazo," the commander's fine manners shroud a dark side that echoes his entirely fictional demise. The new Piedras is a liar who abuses his command position in an attempt to remove a personal rival, a view of Piedras that is common today. This Piedras would be willing to cause his rival's death while lacking the courage to challenge him directly.

The story's imaginative ending may be the first political act of a young author caught up in the angry mood generated by the odious Mexican law. Publishing the exotic tale with revolutionary allusions and overtones may be Pavie's consolation for not participating directly in the "three glorious days" of France's July Revolution. Like other writers fighting with pen instead of sword, he may be suggesting a way for Texans to handle the Mexican authorities who reneged on the bargain they struck, as Piedras reneges on granting Antonio the prize he wins in a fair competition. "Le Lazo" may also be the thrilled expression of enchantment and attraction to danger felt by a young man reared on brigand literature. Pavie's strong sense of decorum, cultivated by his father and grandmother in the combined Pavie household and press, may have caused him to omit Piedras's name in the first publication, which preceded news of the Battle of Nacogdoches. Or the names may be no more than the opportunistic borrowing by a budding linguist of exotic names: Antonio, who sang *romanzas,* won horse races, and had to escape across the Sabine, or don Piedras, who for Pavie represented the aristocratic arrogance of the Spanish Creole during the waning months of Mexican East Texas.

A MEXICAN TALE

The drums were beating the final rolls of the retreat, and the shrill voice of the fifes mingled with the solemn beat of the march. When the little troop of musicians paraded in front of the bench on which Colonel don Piedras was seated, the drum major lifted his cane baton up to the height of his black mustache. Instantly one heard the resounding patriotic tune of the new republic: "Viva la Libertad!"

The colonel rose respectfully, even throwing away his cigarette as he blew out his last puff of smoke. All who made up his staff, from his aides-de-camp in their braid-trimmed hats and shiny belts to the chaplain whose rosary ended in two carved ivory skulls, bowed respectfully. The soldiers crowded into the vast hangar that served as a temporary church. At the drumroll ending the march, each soldier knelt in his row in a pious meditation, and a confused murmur of grave and fervent voices announced that the bronze-faced infantrymen leaning on their muskets had forgotten the forests and their dangers. At the same instant, the sound of the trumpet resounded at the other end of the village. One could hear sabers dragging heavily on the ground and spurs with large rowels jangling on the cavalrymen's boots. After this din of the barracks, the most profound silence followed the prayers recited by the brigadier on duty, repeated in chorus by all the cavalrymen.

When the evening prayer ended, a large fire was lighted at the door of each of the barracks. The sight offered by this village—or rather this "post," as the inhabitants called it—was so strange, so new for a European, that the one who happened across it in the course of his travels could not resist describing it. A double row of low houses, constructed of earth and covered with shingles of cypress bark, comprises the entire hamlet. At the end of the plaza stands a hangar built in the same manner but capped by a bizarre little bell tower whose point—half Gothic, half Moorish—breaks the monotony of the neighboring forests, just as the palm of the oasis balances its animated front in the breast of the immobile desert. The hangar serves as the church, the barracks, and often even the hospital when the August sun sucks up the last drop of water under the shelter of the sugarcane stalks, leaving for men and beasts of the forest only an infested breath that dries the leaves of the catalpas and magnolias. Then the animals flee toward the prairies of the west, and the inhabitants camp under the pines of the highlands. Soldiers who painfully cross these deserts, where withered grasses are reduced to dust, fall exhausted here and there. Their corpses are quickly devoured by starving vultures, leaving sad signposts of bleached bones for those who want to venture across these desolate places.

[That night,] directly across from the main entrance on the spacious plaza, infantrymen had built an immense fire. Its flames, nourished by sweet-gum roots,[10] cast bluish reflections on the steel bayonets and illuminated the interiors of the drums, cymbals, and the *pavillons chinois*.[11] The sentry was immobile, leaning on his gun, his legs crossed in the stance of an ancient Moor to whom the guarding of Grenada had been entrusted. Sometimes one could see him come and go in great strides; in the middle of the silence of the night, his opaque shadow extended to the depths of the hangar and seemed, by its regular oscillations, to be the pendulum of an immense clock. The infantrymen were lying down or seated on logs around the fire. A swirl of smoke spiraling above their heads masked the vault of the sky and the sparkle of the stars, so dazzling in these southern climes.

A few steps from this first bivouac, on a plaza that opened directly onto the forest, burned another, more ardent fire, but one whose flames, compressed by the breeze, which was stronger in this less sheltered place, cast little light and quickly devoured the resinous pines that the cavalrymen threw on them. The men were all around the fire, standing, wrapped in large blue coats thrown back over their shoulders, the characteristic attribute of all who speak the Spanish language. Their heads were covered with ample gray felt hats decorated with black bands and eagle feathers. Some of them poked at the fire with sticks of shiny-leafed laurel (magnolia) and chatted aloud; others sang a romanza accompanied by a Spanish mandolin, and their songs, alternately gay and melancholy, rhythmic and languorous, blended with the hooting of the owl, the cry of the whippoorwill, and the cooing of the wood pigeon in the solitude of the forest. The old cavalrymen, born in the colony and hardened to the climate and the dangers peculiar to this remote region, were gravely draped in coats that extended to the rowels of their spurs. They rolled tobacco in leaves of corn, pulled yams out from under the coals, and told of their combat with the Cherokee Indians and the Karankawas of the desert. This group of Mexicans, in all the purity of their costumes and their habits, presented a sight full of originality—a bit of Spain plus the imposing physiognomy of America, that vague idea of infinity which, in these profoundly silent forests, emanates from everywhere like another atmosphere. Downwind of the fire, on the side made uncomfortable for the cavalrymen by wafting smoke, sat an Indian of the ancient tribe of the Delawares, the latest castaways washed up on the banks who carried their name deep into Texas. Since nightfall, this Indian had done nothing but fill and smoke his pipe. It was impossible to read on his tattooed face what had drawn him to this village. Among his people all he needed to say as he seated himself in a hut was "I am come," and the Indian living in it would answer, presenting him with a gourd filled with water, "Stranger, you are welcome." He was squatting with his weapons nearby, his head hidden by his coat, through which the barrel of his rifle peeked. Everything indicated that the foxy savage leaning on his weapon did so from his people's habit of keeping watch at night around their own bivouacs.

Little by little, cavalrymen and foot soldiers fell asleep on the ground. The Indian stretched out on a buffalo skin, but it would have taken a more skillful eye than a European's to know if his fiery eyes also closed. The sentry, leaning against one of the pillars holding up the hangar, seemed to abandon himself to a profound reverie. An imposing silence reigned in the village and the desert. Anyone who crossed the forest at such an hour would have encountered the last flames of a camp of Choctaws or Coshattas sleeping on the banks of the Sabine, a lost hunter taking cover in a cane hedge, a wildcat with its shrill cry balancing on the branches of a persimmon tree, or even, in the paths of the marshes, a lost alligator far from its lake, instinctively driven to hunt for muddy water.

Suddenly a young cavalryman stood up tall in the midst of the soldiers and slipped like a ghost across his sleeping companions. He was so discreet and nimble that his foot skimmed across all of these faces without betraying his flight. The cavalryman stopped each second to see if the others were sound asleep; he crouched down at the least movement, ready to throw himself to the ground if someone caught him. Step by step he followed his hazardous route, his anxious face moving from side to side and his eyes sparkling. But when he was no longer afraid, when he had crossed the final limits of the camp, he promptly plunged into the forest.

A last stolen glance at the village showed him the post in the same repose; the flames cast only a doubtful light. Never had soldiers rested better by the fire of a bivouac; only one thing seemed to move in the middle of this deep calm. Perhaps a cavalryman had turned over while dreaming, or perhaps the Indian. . . . But what difference could it make? The young Mexican, still breathless from so much tension, inhaled deeply to restore himself after such a long strain. Then he put his noisy spurs back on his boots, threw his coat back over his shoulder, adjusted his scarlet belt and his ivory-handled dagger and, quietly humming a Spanish love song, he moved off like a shot. He caused the shrubs to bend slightly, but the lightness of his journey scarcely left a footprint.

He was a young cavalryman who had already distinguished himself several times in attacks on Indians and, more recently, on the Spanish, near Veracruz.

The day he had arrived with the escort squadron from San Antonio, a young girl from the village was standing in the main plaza amid the scattered groups of Creole planters whose caravan was bringing money from the harvests sold on the Brazos and the Trinity Rivers. Although born in the burning climate of Coahuila, the girl had a light brown tint to her cheeks that lent her the freshness of a rose in the midst of the rough, harsh faces of the Mexicans. She was in the first age when the soul, so pure, so full of harmonious thoughts, is completely reflected in the timidity of the glance; she had the beauty of a charming flower beginning to bloom. Brought up in the depths of the forest alone with her old father, she instinctively felt the burden of the solitude surrounding her; but a vague desire to animate this solitude, an irresistible need to concentrate on a worthy being the love that she accorded to each object of creation, infused a sweet melancholy into her reveries. In the evenings when the old colonist sat on the threshold of his door, wrapped in his striped mantle and smoking with pleasure, the young girl silently turned the rosary in her fingers, casting an ecstatic gaze on the setting sun, which tinted the flowering magnolia pink. She prayed ardently, and then the handsome cavalryman passed by in his brilliant uniform. Antonio loved Clara with all the strength of his soul, and when the squadron of horsemen paraded their horses in the field, Clara's two black eyes were always fastened on Antonio.

That very night he was going to say his good-byes to the colonist and his daughter. The next day there was going to be a horse race, and in a few days he would have to leave on an expedition. With the agility of an Indian, the Mexican traversed the distance separating him from the old man's dwelling; he leapt across the lianas tangled under his feet, ran, flew with ever increasing impatience, and a feeling of happiness made his heart beat violently. As he was hurrying along in the forest, preoccupied with his thoughts, something opaque—a shadow—slipped between the trees, and the noise of a footstep sounded on the dry grass. Antonio quickened his pace, then stopped and cautiously came back. . . . It was the braided uniform, the brown coat, the elegant feather, the white sombrero of the colonel himself. A sudden jealousy inflamed the heart of the young cavalryman; his hand reached for his dagger. Immobile, overtaken by an uncontrollable fury, he was going to throw himself on his chief and annihilate him. "But, no," he said to himself, "I will find out everything and, if necessary, I will avenge myself."

Then he followed his enemy closely; all his hopes were turned upside down when the colonel proceeded to Clara's house. What did he want? What led him there? Because Antonio had failed in his duty by leaving his barracks for a nocturnal rendezvous, all he could do was spy on the path of don Piedras with jealous attention and try to discern his intentions.

The colonel knocked softly at the door of the cabin. Antonio, leaning on the other end of the house, was no longer breathing; one would have taken him for one of those old poplar trees struck down by lightning. There was a movement inside, a sound of footsteps, and a soft voice that asked, "Is that you, Antonio?"

The young man jumped at this call. The colonel muttered between his teeth, then announced out loud, "Open, my child, I am don Piedras, don Piedras, the commander."

"What! You! Such an honor, señor Colonel!" the old man cried, giving his seat to his guest.

And he begged him to be seated near the fire. Clara took her place beside her father in an angle of the chimney and, lifting her mantilla over her head to envelop the lower half of her face, she remained silent, leaning on her hands. A green parrot, balancing himself on the can strips of the floor, traveled along a stalk to place himself familiarly on her shoulder.

There was a moment of silence.

"Antonio has conducted himself badly toward us," don Piedras finally said, trying to steady his voice, and he looked around, feeling vaguely

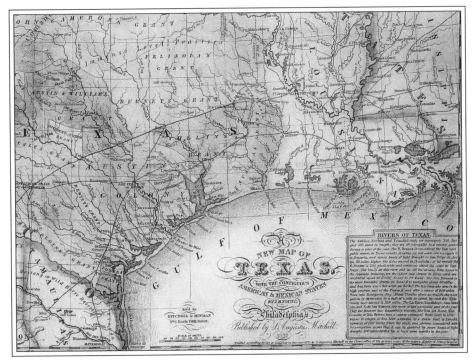

Pavie crossed the Sabine on the Gaines Ferry when traveling between
Natchitoches and Nacogdoches in 1830. "Burnet's Grant" is the land that was in
contention between the Cherokee people and Haden Edwards in 1827. Mexican
officials took it back from Edwards after the Fredonian Rebellion and granted it
to David G. Burnet, future president of the Republic of Texas. *Courtesy Map
Collection, The Center for American History, The University of Texas at Austin
(CN 06014)*

uneasy. "He failed in his duties, his lieutenant denounced him, and he
has set a dangerous example. It is for us to use our power and punish him
according to the laws. I know, venerable old man, and you, young lady,
the interest that you have in him—"

And the parrot repeated in the ear of his mistress the name that was so
familiar: "Antonio! Antonio!"

The colonel broke off involuntarily.

"Therefore he should be exiled from this land, exiled for life." And the
piercing eyes of the liar dug like nails into the pale forehead of Clara,
completely vexed. "If more serious punishments are spared him, believe
me, my child," and his voice became caressing, "that it is only for love of

you. As for me, for a long time, I have noticed your attractiveness and charm."

But the young woman turned her back to the colonel. The perfidy in his accent did not escape her candid soul, and, while he was pretending to console the heart he had just mortally wounded, Clara hid her face under her black veil and drew herself into a disdainful silence. Then the parrot repeated the name of Antonio again with a sound that was so imploring and tender that the vexed commander rose, exchanged a few words with the old man, clumsily saluted the indignant young woman, and disappeared, disconcerted and ashamed but certain of having dispensed with his rival. The old colonist was so baffled by this strange visit that at daybreak he was still in the same place, his eyes fastened on the half-burned logs as if he were still listening to the colonel's last words.

"Who goes there?" cried the sonorous voice of Antonio, cocking his carbine.

And don Piedras (for it was he, returning slowly from his excursion) seemed to hesitate at this voice which made him feel guilty.

"Who goes there! Or I swear on St. Anthony, my patron, you are a dead man," the sentry said, pressing the butt of his musket to his shoulder.

"Your colonel," don Piedras responded.

As the cavalryman, trembling with anger, gave his chief the military salute, the carbine rattled violently in his hands. He barely heard the conversation in the cabin when he promptly left to resume his post, and he had not taken two steps into his sentry hut when the colonel reappeared.

"No one was absent tonight? Everything was peaceful in the camp?" the colonel added, casting a questioning glance at the proud head of the soldier on sentry duty.

The brigadier on duty, advancing with his lantern, spared the cavalryman the embarrassment of a response.

After this inspection, the commander left. As he disappeared in the fading light of the dying flame, hidden in his coat like the genie of darkness, Antonio murmured some inaudible words, raised and lowered his weapon, then suddenly threw it down.

"No!" he told himself. "That would be a cowardly betrayal. I'll have my vengeance later!" And he resumed his sentry duty.

Meanwhile, the Indian, whose keen eye had followed all of the movements of the cavalryman that night, stood up quietly after the colonel left and caught up with him at the door to the infantrymen's quarters. He responded to the call of the sentry, who was surprised to see him slip like a shadow along the cabins, with the single word "Delaware," pronounced with the Indian stress, placing his left hand on his chest and presenting the palm of his right. The mysterious savage tapped lightly on the shoulder of the chief of the warriors, as he called don Piedras, and led him toward the cavalrymen's fire, always off to the side. Then, directing his attention toward Antonio leaning on his saber in the posture of an active sentry, the Delaware directed his arm toward him, lifted his finger on the forest side toward the place where the moon is at midnight, and remained silent.

"Good, good," the commander murmured. "He followed me, he knows everything. Time presses. He will murder me if I do not kill him first."

He wished to ask the Indian's advice, but the inhabitant of the desert was no longer there. Don Piedras remained alone, preoccupied with his vengeance; he walked in great strides, violently agitated, a serious look on his face. The soldiers, who were beginning to awaken, yawned and asked each other, "Amigo, mira, que tiene pués el señor colonel?" ["Friend, what's wrong with the colonel?"]

Soon, extraordinary activity broke out among them. They polished their rifles, bayonets, and sabers; the drum rolled at intervals, and the instruments summoned them to the barracks. In the camp of the cavalrymen, bridles and bits jangled; sabers sparkled, golden spurs reflected the sun's rays, and the horses, covered with their saddle blankets of buffalo skins stitched in porcupine, snorted impatiently. A sudden fanfare announced the commander's arrival. He advanced proudly on a horse of dazzling whiteness; its mane floated in the wind and covered the golden trim on the bridle. The soldiers swore that his embroidered saddle was worth at least a thousand pesos. The aides-de-camp saluted, bringing their hands up to the eagle feathers in their hats; the chaplain, in military uniform modified in the manner of European clerics, took his place on the left; the ranks formed, and the company started out.

The cavalrymen acted as the advance guard. One of them, Antonio, seemed preoccupied with his horse; his head appeared above those of the other horsemen, rising and falling like a wave undulating on the ocean. On the large plaza, his eyes met Clara's. She was there, her black embroidered mantilla forming a diadem on her forehead and falling in festoons on her shoulders. At the sound of horses, the young woman turned involuntarily, and each soldier could observe in passing that she was speaking into the ear of her father, while he seemed to search for something in the middle of the squadron. Then the colonel appeared, surrounded by his officers in rich uniform, prancing along on their luxuriously bedecked horses. But Clara had fixed her gaze on the group of cavalrymen who were disappearing in a cloud of dust.

In the middle of the field designated for the horse race, the cavalry halted and the infantrymen placed themselves at the far end of the clearing. Four slaves brought out two wild horses, their eyes covered with woolen strips that would not be removed until the instant the race began. When the distances were measured, the judges (the colonel and the head officer) gave the order to begin. Two runners appeared, vigorous Mexicans who were scantily dressed, their hair pulled into Castilian nets. At the sight of Antonio, don Piedras's forehead furrowed; but he leaned toward the Indian, whom no one had noticed arriving at this plaza, and exchanged a few words with his new confidant. Immediately the colonel's face lit up with joy, and he designated for his rival Antonio the steed which seemed the more difficult to break.

"And you believe that he will carry him off into the forest and smash him into the trees?" don Piedras again asked the savage, who answered affirmatively.

Meanwhile the trumpets resounded from the four corners of the racetrack. The two cavalrymen snatched the blindfolds from the steeds and threw themselves like panthers onto their shiny backs. The spectators' cries traveled no more quickly across the space than the two unbroken steeds. At first, only a single dot could be seen flying through the emptiness; then, little by little, when the breeze had dissipated the cloud that so mysteriously enveloped the riders, the two flying Mexicans could be seen, their heads lowered like ostriches fleeing the lances of Indians. In the middle of the race, one of them rolled under the feet of the fiery animal, and a piercing scream broke out in the crowd. Don Piedras's lip curled in a smile of triumph until his glance fell on the Delaware, whose severe expression had not changed. The sweaty rider suddenly passed by; his black hair floated on his neck, his legs along the flanks of the horse bent to the wild movements of the animal. His entire person embodied so much grace and beauty that all forgot the danger of this race to the death and admired the one whom the public voice proclaimed winner.

His arms crossed his heaving chest, disdaining the help of the mane, and he cast a triumphant glance over all the people until he lowered his fiery eyes in front of the timid face of Clara. For the winner was Antonio.

Disconcerted, don Piedras did not know if he should believe his eyes. Anger reddened his bronzed cheeks. Never had a Spanish brow gleamed with such a thirst for vengeance. The conquered horse was brought back out and, on the colonel's orders, the race had to start over again.

A murmur arose from everywhere on the plain; the spectators yelled at the unfairness.

"He was the winner" was repeated. "The prize was won, fair and square."

The colonel's vengeance sought its victim, but it was Antonio who seized the occasion to avenge his anger. The competition started over. The winner, beside himself, fired by his recent glory, his hatred reinvigorated, grabbed hold of the wild horse, and none of the horse's efforts succeeded in throwing him. A lasso whistled like a slingshot around his head. The crowd was astonished; the movements of the rider were fantastic and frightening to witness, and a profound hush fell. Antonio was not a hundred feet from the officer corps; his left hand, leaning heavily on his hatchet, held the end of the rope, and his piercing glance fixed on a single point in the center of the officers. Suddenly the knot vibrated violently and straightened—the lasso had hit its target. His gesture was so rapid that Colonel don Piedras of Santa Fé rolled in the dust, hit the ground, split open his forehead, and left a wide trail of blood in the arena before anyone perceived that there was no longer a rider on the golden blanket covering the white horse.

No one knew what had become of the cavalryman.

Today an elegant cabin rises above the banks of the Sabine, on the American side; there, travelers find a welcoming asylum. In the evening a handsome Mexican can be seen swinging in his hammock, drinking Madeira and smoking Havana cigars while his young wife prepares the meals for strangers; a green parrot is perched on the threshold of the gallery, repeating continuously, "Antonio! Antonio!"

La Peau d'ours

EDITOR'S NOTES

The name "Fredonian Rebellion"[1] is given to events in an East Texas land dispute in late 1826 and early 1827 among Mexican officials, American settlers, and the nearby Cherokees.[2] During this period, numerous adventurers and malcontents, remnants of failed filibustering expeditions, also filled the Nacogdoches region, where the Mexican government granted land to Haden Edwards to settle up to eight hundred American colonists. This grant was in a contentious location west of the former Neutral Ground, north of the Austin colony, and south of the Cherokees who had come to Texas in 1819 and 1820 with the informal approval of the Mexican officials. The government wanted to establish a buffer zone of Indians between the United States and their fledgling country.

A principal party to the dispute was Richard Fields, a mixed-race (one-eighth) Cherokee chief who spoke English and had become a master Mason in Mexico City in 1823.[3] He began to call himself "captain general of the Indian tribes in the province of Texas," stating that the superior government had granted him "territory sufficient for me and that part of the tribe dependent upon me to settle on, and also a commission to command all the Indian tribes and nations that are in the four eastern provinces."[4] His aggressive organizing of the Indians in Texas began to threaten the Mexican authorities. When he refused to submit to local authority in 1825,[5] officials in Mexico City denied that documents existed supporting a commission for Fields or a land grant for his people. Furthermore, they instructed the local authorities to prevent him from assembling his tribes.[6] Claims for the Cherokee land were further clouded by the general colonization law of 1824, which caused an influx of Anglo Americans in 1825.

Throughout the late summer of 1826, red and white settlers alike were in what Dianna Everett characterizes as "a very troubled and nervous state." Rumors, fed by Fields himself, predicted an imminent attack by Comanches. Fields wrote Stephen F. Austin around September 5, 1826, that the Comanches planned to "attack your colony and destroy it entirely, or compel the settlers to leave it by the beginning of the next moon."[7] He sent a similar message to the Nacogdoches alcalde, at the same time requesting permission to make war on the Comanches who had, according to Fields, killed some of his people.

Haden Edwards, also designated by the Mexicans to colonize the region, had been required to uphold all previous grants, whether Spanish or Mexican. Frustrated by the resulting ambiguities in titles and claims, Haden and his brother Benjamin (the opportunistic Edwards brothers) organized a revolt against the Mexican government, counting on the fighting strength of the disgruntled Cherokees and their Indian allies. Benjamin Edwards signed an agreement with Fields in December, 1826, so that "their united effort will be immediately directed against this base and faithless government."[8] Calling their nation Fredonia, the rebels declared their independence from Mexico and flew a flag proclaiming "Independence, Liberty, and Justice" over the Old Stone Fort that became their "capitol.". . . a mere three years before Pavie stayed there with the Durst!

In late December, (1826), the Fredonians appealed to Austin and his colonists to join them, but Austin sided with the Mexican authorities, who dispatched troops from San Antonio. By now the Mexicans—generally uncertain of the Indians' loyalties—were concerned about the possibility of a total conflagration. Winkler describes the near-hysterical climate among the provincial military: "Their disturbed imaginations pictured every Indian in Texas in arms ready to strike the frontier at every point, and soldiers flocking to the Fredonian standard in such numbers that they must number 1,000 very shortly."[9] One Mexican counterrevolutionary strategy—divide and conquer—launched by the experienced Colonel Peter Ellis Bean, an Indian agent for the Mexican government, was to create dissension within the Cherokee confederation by promising land to other chiefs such as Bowles and Big Mush. On January 4, 1827, Bean wrote to Austin, "I wish you to hurry on the troops as fast as Posibel for now is our time Before the ingins geather."[10]

Bean's tactic worked. Mexican troops, supported by Austin and a mounted militia, were dispatched from San Antonio to Nacogdoches. When Fields tried to muster his Cherokee allies against these loyalist forces, he discovered that Bean and his agents had been to the Cherokee village and promised them the land for which they contended. Cherokees under Bowles and Big Mush murdered Fields and presented the Fredonian flag to the Mexican officials as a gesture of loyalty. This incident effectively eliminated the Cherokees as allies to the Fredonians, who were unable to fight by themselves. The Fredonian rebels left Nacogdoches on December 28, 1826, crossing the Sabine shortly afterward. The Mexican government sent troop reinforcements to Nacogdoches under the command of José de las Piedras, and the town was secured for five years until the Battle of Nacogdoches on August 2, 1832, which resulted in the removal of Mexican troops from East Texas. Despite his advanced age, Bowles tried to come to the aid of Piedras with a band of warriors, but the Cherokees arrived too late to help their Mexican allies.[11] The polite Piedras, a Centralist, was demonized by Americans in Texas for refusing to support their Federalist choice for Mexican leader, Santa Anna.

GROUPS REPRESENTED BY THE CHARACTERS

Texas' unstable political situation intensified the elemental fear within the human heart, and this fear is given literary expression in Pavie's story. Fear drives the action in "La Peau d'ours" ("The Bearskin") after the reader meets a comfortable array of characters who embody the diverse cultures of the late 1820s Natchitoches community.

The characters act out several typical methods of frontier land acquisition. Old planters received land grants, some colonists purchased their land, and settlers known in Louisiana as *petits blancs* "squatted" on their land. Native Americans are presented singly, in pairs, or en masse when they arrive in Natchitoches for their gifts from the Indian agent. They are being pushed ahead of the settlers. Traders arrive by boat or ox train, or on foot or horseback. Though Louisiana had already achieved statehood, most of the characters are French of language and heart. Thirty years before, in *Souvenirs atlantiques*,[12] Pavie had noted that although power belongs to the conqueror, "there remains in the depths of the soul of a population which has changed only its name, the same feelings of affection and hatred. . . . We are still French." The view he expressed in

1861 in "La Peau d'ours" had sobered: "these people and their descendants obstinately call themselves Canadians, which in their minds means French, and for the most part they still speak the language of the country that has so completely forgotten them." Having settled in Louisiana earlier than the Canadian and his sons, the planter and his daughter are totally assimilated into the local society.

Hospitable and somewhat headstrong, Marie, who decorates her party gown with feathers, represents young, single Creole women. Possessing some equestrian skills, she nonetheless depends on a kinsman (husband, father, or brother) for safety. The stable planter class, represented by Marie's father, enjoyed great material and social privileges. Though European, her father plays an important role in the local culture.

Père Faustin, a Canadian, seems to represent any number of political or economic exiles who selected Louisiana because of its French language and culture and its frontier opportunities. Although a friendship of long date implies that Faustin had been rowing Louisiana rivers as early as the eighteen-teens, his sons may have participated in the Canadian fur trade. Economic and cultural pressures on French Canadians had steadily increased since the 1821 consolidation of Canada's two rival fur companies, the North West Company and the Hudson's Bay Company. Canadian Governor George Simpson's reorganization of the fur industry around the newly expanded Hudson's Bay Company eliminated the role of French traders and merchants.[13] For a short while, displaced Canadian oarsmen could find work on U.S. rivers, but this employment disappeared precipitously as steamers increased. Returning to Canada would have been undesirable by 1826, when politicians introduced legislation to restrict the French language and the practice of Catholicism.[14] Like his sons Antoine and Étienne, typical of the eternal "younger generation," Faustin is fiercely independent.

The solitary savage, skillful, resourceful, and sensitive when not inebriated, represents the Native Americans displaced by rapid population growth in the eastern United States. Isolated and addicted to alcohol at worst, he can still outrun and outwit three white men in the forest when sober.

Finally, nature appears in a variety of roles. Nature is Mother Earth, nourishing her children with crops and game. Rivers provide transportation, and trees provide shelter. The bear sacrifices its skin, which becomes a blanket. This skin is also the central metaphor for vanishing resources as the frontier moves westward—resources for which a diverse and growing population will compete.

BIOGRAPHICAL ELEMENTS

The villainous savage appears to be a composite of several Native Americans that Pavie described in *Souvenirs atlantiques,* including a young man who was so proud of a facial scar that he tattooed red and blue around it and wore his hair in a "hoope tuft" (standing straight up) to display it better. Pavie had frequent contact with members of several tribes close to Natchitoches and Campti (where the Pavie plantation was located), in addition to his memorable Nacogdoches encounter with Bowles and his Cherokee followers.

Charles Pavie provided the model for the planter, and his adopted daughter, Marie Elisa Bludworth, inspired Marie.[15] Marianne Pavie died in 1834; her absence is also reflected in the characterization. Other autobiographical elements from the author's American experience, many of which appear in *Souvenirs atlantiques,* are played out by various characters. For example Pavie reported great fear when he was lost in a forest on July 2, 1829. Antoine's shyness in the wedding setting is reminiscent of Pavie's reports of being unwilling to attend a ball in his cousin's honor. When he returned to France, he confessed his love for Elisa, his Creole cousin, to his brother. Did Pavie's reminiscences form the basis of the tender and clumsy love between Antoine and Marie, snuffed out prematurely by the fate of Antoine's father?[16]

I

Canadians have ventured into the most remote parts of America, wherever there are rivers or streams capable of carrying a pirogue. Their robust constitution makes them well suited for braving the most extreme climates: they can endure the rigors of a winter's cold on the banks of Lake Huron and the energy-sapping heat of southern Louisiana with the same courage, or rather with the same indifference. The four rivers these indefatigable Northerners frequented most willingly were the St. Lawrence, the Ohio, the Missouri, and the Mississippi. New Orleans attracted great numbers of those nomadic rowers, who came to enlist as sailors in the service of merchants known as caboteurs. The caboteurs ascended the rivers of Louisiana in large barques to sell shoddy goods imported from France and England. These wholesale peddlers were Europeans, especially Frenchmen, who had come to America to make their fortunes. Peddling along the waterways, and often quite far inland, offered them a sure means of achieving their goal. This trade, however, had its fatigues, dangers, and tedium. The traveler had to struggle against wasting heat, yellow fever, and sometimes epidemics as well. Smallpox, for example, which in the past had decimated the indigenous populations, continued to break out often among the crews, forcing the barque to stop along the route. Canadians, usually such calm and resigned oarsmen, were nonetheless independent and volatile. An inopportune reprimand or a hurried meal was all that was needed to provoke these not entirely docile rowers. Despite such conflicts and difficulties, however, the caboteur patiently endured, for indeed, there were compensations. In the habitations he approached to sell his wares, his presence caused a general joy. He was welcomed and received with acts of kindness because the majority of the rich planters had also begun as caboteurs. Yet their familiarity with his ways did not protect them or their families from letting themselves be taken in by the babble and tempting offers of the traveling salesman. This fellow had the right to be seated at the hospitable table of the planter. After dinner, when he had amused the women and children with his stories, the caboteur would open his bundles, always reserving his most beautiful wares for last. Thus, when the planter's family had bought the essential household articles, they might still give in to the desire to acquire some superfluities. Having concluded his deal, the caboteur would pack his bags as slowly as possible while spouting forth the latest news. Oh! He knew so much of it! Then, the following day, at the moment of departure, he would suddenly remember, as if by chance, a particular rich and tasteful adornment that he had kept carefully hidden in a corner of his cabin. A new temptation for the young ladies! The caboteur—with one foot on the shore and the other on board the barque—cleverly cast his final net. Indulgently, he stopped his rowers, who were on the verge of setting sail, to discuss hurriedly the price of these desired objects. As for payment, each customer complied with the custom of the times: in cash and on the spot, or double and in kind at the next harvest. The merchant thus scattered, with great profit to himself, all along the rivers of Louisiana, masses of outdated articles that no one in Europe any longer wanted at any price. When he had exhausted his stock of shoddy goods, he would go back down the river, filling the empty hold of his barque along the route with his return cargo of cotton bales and barrels of sugar. Little by little the barque was refilled, and the current of the Mississippi gently conducted the refreshed crew and the enriched owner back to the quays of New Orleans. Steamers killed this small commerce a little at a time; the masters of the barques became planters and merchants. Many years ago now, I saw the last boats of the caboteurs, run aground on the shores and abandoned!

Among the rowers, those who had the foresight to amass some savings went to the southern and western states to buy land. Those who possessed nothing moved ahead, exploring the forests, living off game, cultivating here and there a few feet of corn in imperfectly plowed clearings, and then advancing further, caught between the Americans who completely cleared the land and the savages who retreated before them. There were those who lived among the Indians in the manner of pigeons that happen to mix with passenger pigeons. Wherever they are found, in U.S. territory or the British possessions, in the provinces of old or New Mexico, these people and their descendants obstinately call themselves Canadians, which, in their minds, means French, and for the most part they still speak the language of the country that has so completely forgotten them. What distinguishes these knights errant of the desert from American pioneers is that, instead of marching together and head on like the latter, they move ahead separately as solitary scouts.

At the time when the caboteurs were abandoning the navigation of the rivers of Louisiana, some time in the 1820s, a large pirogue propelled by three rowers was seen arriving at Natchitoches, the last village [in the United States] one encountered when going westward on the Red River. They rowed like people accustomed to traveling on rivers, striking the water in cadence with their short paddles and gliding straight ahead, from one spit of land to another, without following the capricious contours of the banks. The sun had just risen; it was springtime, and the slopes were covered with that cheerful greenery that the summer sun withers so quickly. That particular morning a lot of people were on the quay. Letters and newspapers, delivered the night before by mail, were being distributed, and the planters of the neighborhood, seated on wooden benches in the shade of flowering black locust trees in front of the shops, chatted and smoked their cigars. Negroes noisily rolled down the dock the goods which heavy carts hitched to three or four pairs of oxen were bringing from the interior of Mexico.[17] The people of color, no doubt to make their masters understand that they had burdened them with too heavy a load, could not move without screaming, howling, and struggling like souls in torment. Here and there in the crowd one also saw several Indians who had come to town with the spoils of their hunt. They had nothing left to do, for the market hour had passed and they had sold their game, but they remained there idly, squatting in the shade before the houses, silent, their eyes half-closed like vultures who have had their meal and are resting. They belonged to the tribes scattered far from there in Arkansas, but they hardly ever lived with the families of their nation. They spent their time prowling around the habitations and pursuing large and small game in the neighboring forests, just like those birds of prey who, accustomed to perching on an old tree, do not even move away when the work of clearing has felled the surrounding woods. They were like the stragglers of those savage hordes that civilization pushed aside.

There were therefore, that morning, on the quay of Natchitoches, a goodly number of whites, Negroes, and Indians; and, just as when one is at the edge of a river one watches it flow despite oneself, the eyes of everyone there turned toward the approaching pirogue.[18] When it landed, those who had been on board headed toward a tavern to fill their jugs. By their great stature, their pale complexions, and their long black hair, everyone recognized them immediately as Canadians. People pressed around them with a certain interest, for there were among them more than one small merchant, settled in America for scarcely two or three years, who held it against the steamboats that they were not yet millionaires. Some saw these rowers who had been forced into retirement as victims of an innovation they themselves disliked; others recognized former colleagues whom they did not ever remember having seen but whom they must have met a hundred times. The tavern where the Canadians stopped was soon filled with idlers thirsting to hear some news and tell some of their own. Others lingered in the doorway, and soon it was learned officially on the quay that these three travelers were a father and his two sons—once sailors on the caboteurs of the Mississippi, forced out of work like so many others. They had come to the region to settle, and they spoke of settling fifteen or twenty leagues from the small town, beyond the most remote houses.

While this news, quite important in a locale where scarcely any arrived, was circulating among the crowd, the Canadians clinked glasses with all those who poured rum for them. And when they decided to get back under way, their faces were quite animated.

"Father," the elder son said, stretching his long, robust arms like an athlete who needs exercise, "let's go! The air of the river will be better for us than this tavern, where my head is beginning to spin."

"In our day," the father said, addressing several old Creoles yellowed by the sun and whitened by age, "it took more than this to blur the vision of a rower of the St. Lawrence!" And he rose suddenly. After shaking the hands of those who surrounded him, wishing him a good journey, he signaled his younger son to walk ahead of him. Faithful to this custom of always staying in single file, which they had borrowed from the savages, they majestically crossed the square, *following each other like cranes and goslings,* according to the simple but accurate expression of an old traveler.

Just as they were approaching their pirogue, they saw an Indian carefully examining it. The Canadians had laid out their long rifles, axes, powder horns, and other hunting tools there. These riches dazzled the savage; whose own rifle was a pitiful, shabby arm, worn out by twenty years of service and completely patched. Bent over on the shore of the river, his arms crossed, his neck stretched like a spaniel at point, he watched with the intensity of contemplation that civilized man knows not.

"Watch out!" the youngest of the three Canadians yelled at him. "Get away from there so we can get back on board."

And as he said this, his older brother, who was following him closely, gave the savage a violent shove with his shoulder. The Indian lost his balance, let out a cry of distress and anger, and, rather than let himself belly flop into the river, dived in with his head lowered; his dog leapt forward in his wake as if to search for his master under the water. Several seconds later the Indian reappeared on shore, soiled with mud. The red and blue paint that tattooed his face streamed in large drops down his cheeks and onto his bare chest. At the sight of this body so strangely mottled, emerging from the bosom of the waves like a river god, the idlers gathered on the quay burst out laughing and clapped their hands, the Negroes howled with joy, and the children threw stones. The village dogs, excited by the cries of the crowd, launched themselves in pursuit of the wet dog, who thus had his share in his master's misadventure. The Indian, to protect himself from their bites, performed pirouettes, twisting and leaping, and distributed kicks of his heel to the gaping jaws of the mastiffs and mongrels. These bizarre leaps gave him the appearance of a maniac and a madman. His retreat was, therefore, in all respects a shameful escape. Finally man and beast, shamed and ridiculed, disappeared into the woods surrounding the town. Once he was at the summit of a hill where the view stretches as far as the Red River, the savage stopped, stroked his dog, and dried himself in the tall grasses, wallowing there like a wounded boar. While he was drying himself in the sun he caught sight of the three Canadians' pirogue disappearing under the gigantic sycamore trees whose dense branches hung over the waters, projecting huge shadows.

In the small town people had laughed about the misfortune of the Indian, it is true; this incident came at just the right moment to delight the inhabitants, already excited by the arrival of the strangers! Even so, there was more than one charitable soul who disapproved of the young rower's violence. The wisest claimed that this act of brutality indicated inborn meanness. This question was discussed for the rest of the day; and in the evening, among those who had hooted at the savage some could be found who, nodding their heads, said, "He's a bad one, the big Canadian!"

II

Rested by their stop at the tavern and enlivened by a sufficient number of glasses of rum, the Canadians set out again with renewed enthusiasm. Clutching their short pipes in their teeth, they rowed as if they were trying to win the regatta prize and put into practice the adage of their country: one never works better than for oneself. During their rapid journey, they passed pretty houses surrounded by rich farms, behind which they heard, through the thickets, the lowing of cattle and the whinnying of horses. The Negroes, busy hoeing the cotton fields, stopped for an instant to see the light pirogue cutting through the water, and the Canadians shot along like the bird that flies straight to the forest. Hunger began to pursue them, however, and just as they noticed a nicely shaded island where they could cook at their leisure the slices of dried meat they had brought with them, a voice from the shore cried out to them, "Hey! In the pirogue!"

At this unexpected shout, the rowers raised their heads and remained motionless, paddles in hand.

"Is it you, père Faustin?" continued the same voice.[19]

Hearing someone call his name, the old Canadian craned his head toward shore. His two sons pointed out a planter seated by the water; he held a telescope trained on the barque and signaled to them to approach by waving his large palm-leaf hat. The Canadians turned the prow in his direction, and, before setting foot on the land, père Faustin recognized this planter as a former merchant of Lower Louisiana with whom he had long sailed.[20] This encounter was nothing out of the ordinary. The Red River, bordered by extremely fertile land that in places was still covered by vast forests, at that time attracted great numbers of caboteurs who had been forced to give up their business. They came to settle around the villages where succeeding generations of French Creoles lived happily and tranquilly, passing their lands from father to son. The American element that would later overflow into this little colony was hardly noticeable; it was a world apart, where the simple and hospitable customs of our colonists were preserved in their primitive naïveté. The planter exchanged cordial handshakes with the Canadians and invited them to stop for a rest in his habitation.[21] As they walked, they told each other what had happened since their last encounter. Between the retired caboteur and the sailors of the pirogue, distance was erased by the equality of color, the latter being as pure white as the former. The planter's possessions consisted of a fine expanse of land—woods, lakes, and savannahs—in the middle of which man's hand had carved out fields. Tree trunks, still standing and blackened by smoke, indicated that the clearing dated back only a few years. At the center of this half-wild domain stood the residence of the owner, a simple wood house covered with cypress[22] bark and surrounded by a spacious courtyard that served as a paddock for horses. From the back of the courtyard, a rather wide path extended to the forest, while a gently sloping stock path led to the water where flimsy pirogues and large flat-bottomed barques were moored. The barques, built for transporting to the mill the cotton harvested on the opposite shore, were covered with racks made of reeds, which gave them the appearance of floating cages. At the edge of the water, the shacks of the Negroes formed a small hamlet sheltered by a canopy of maples and sycamores.

"What luck, père Faustin," the planter said as he invited the Canadians to come in. "What luck that I was there with my spyglass keeping an eye on my lazy blacks who were digging on the other side of the river! You would have passed in front of a friend's house without knowing it. Ah, père Faustin, in the days when we sailed together, there was money to be earned all along the rivers!"

"And today the best rower on the St. Lawrence would not find enough to purchase his bread," the old man replied, seating himself at the table, where appetizing slices of venison glistened; then he drew a long knife from a leather sheath in his belt and began to eat. His sons followed suit; absorbed by the important task that engaged their attention, the three Canadians did not raise their eyes from their plates. The young slaves responsible for serving watched with stupefaction as these athletically built strangers ate with their hats on their heads and seemed determined not to leave the smallest scrap—which the children coveted. Toward the end of the meal the planter's daughter entered. At a sign from her father, she brought out a flask of wild cherry liqueur, and, seeing at a glance that she was dealing with guests little accustomed to the ways of the world, she attempted, half out of curiosity, half out of mischief, to extract a few words from them. She asked them if they were going very far.

"That depends," the old man replied. "We plan on going out beyond the last habitation. We're going to settle in the woods, we are."

"It seems there are deer around here," said Antoine, the elder of the two sons, as he pushed the plate—from which he had just taken the last slice of venison—back to the middle of the table. "Are there also bear?"

"Bear?" the young girl replied, crossing her little arms and giving her voice an intonation as serious as it was ironic. "Bear? Well, some do stop by here . . . occasionally."

At this answer, in which the tall Canadian had not sensed even the shadow of malice, Étienne, the younger of the two brothers, turned slowly and gave the Creole's daughter a look that made her blush. The planter, taking his turn addressing his guests, tried to make them understand that it would be more advantageous to them to stay in the neighborhood instead of disappearing into the forest. He would give them good cornfields to cultivate; with his help they could more easily clear a certain number of acres, and later they could buy some blacks and would rank among those called by the name of "habitants" [planters]. Hearing this proposition, the old Canadian shook his head, Antoine pouted, and Étienne lowered his eyes.

"Well then," the planter resumed, "I can see quite well that you are men of the wilderness. Let us discuss it no more. If it's the forest you need, you will find it several leagues from here, as isolated as you could wish it. Live there then as you see fit, and, in case you should change your mind, remember that I am always ready to build you a cabin on my land."

"Thanks a lot!" said the elder Faustin. "When you want some nice piece of game, you have only to say the word. We're well rested now, and, with your permission, we're going to get back on our way."

With that, they left. "Mr. Antoine," the young Creole girl called out as their barque moved away, "I forgot to tell you that you will find turkey hens on the river islands and quite a lot of tortoises on the shores!"

Antoine, who had turned around, replied with a nod of his head accompanied by this simple word: "Good!" And the young girl burst out laughing.

"Marie," her father said, "what pleasure do you take in making fun of these simple people? Their life has been spent in hard work. They are a bit crude, but sincere and good-hearted."

"I'm not making fun of them, Father," Marie answered. "They asked me for information which I'm quite proud to be able to give them."

Speaking thus, she took her father's arm and they returned to the house. The Canadians were already far away. After rowing the rest of the day, they camped on the shore, and the next day they began to explore the promised land they had come so far to find. The fields of corn cultivated by the petits blancs[23] followed the cotton plantations. Little by little, caiman appeared in greater numbers on the shores; the turkeys wandering in flocks in the high grasses of the savannahs and under the willows of the islands seemed less afraid of the sound of oars; parrots, gathered in innumerable flocks,[24] made the woods ring with their hoarse and discordant cries. At these signs of a less disturbed solitude, the Canadians understood that they were coming to the end of their journey. They turned the prow of their pirogue toward shore and set off with their weapons and bags toward the highlands—called thus in contrast to the lowlands and alluvium. For the site of their establishment they chose a hill covered with sassafras midway between the Red River and the Sabine, a small, steep-banked river whose murky and rapid waters separate Louisiana from Texas.[25] The banks of the Red River would have offered them a richer soil and more picturesque sites, but they feared the fevers associated with humid places subject to flooding. Moreover, they were not about to plant sugarcane or sow cotton, and poetry was not their affair.

No, certainly these rustic children of America understood nothing about poetry, but they had the instinct of that powerful nature, which drew them toward solitude. When they had taken possession of their

Unafraid of man or beast, the Canadians feared the "fevers" associated with picturesque landscapes like the one Pavie captured in his sketch of *Lac de la Terre Noire,* today Lake Sibley. Avoiding land fertilized by seasonal flooding, they settled midway between the Red River and the Sabine. *Sketch by Théodore Pavie, 1829–30. Courtesy Chasle Pavie Collection*

hill, the old Canadian, shaking his whitened head, breathed in deeply the intense and penetrating forest air and spoke to his two sons: "Now, my boys, axes in hand, let's build!" He set to clearing the soil of the undergrowth that obstructed his way while his two sons went to fell with their axes the age-old trees that grew freely on the slope of the hill. For several days the echo of their axes resounded—a labor of ruin and destruction, whatever one may say, and which saddens the soul! Seeing these gigantic trees fall to the ground, these "kings of the forest," as Hindu poets call them, one imagines despite oneself that nevermore will such trees grow! The log house[26] was soon built on the solitary hill far enough from any other house that the Canadians could not see the smoke of a neighboring roof appearing through the foliage. They were delighted at the thought that they would have elbow room to hunt. The hunter is like the bird of prey, which can bear no individual of its own species in its vicinity.

III

It would be a mistake to believe that the love of order and regular work that inspires the farmers of the northern United States was the dominant passion of our Canadians. Despite the fact that several feet of tobacco, corn, and sweet potatoes grew around their cabin, these results were more attributable to the fertile soil and mild climate than to the immigrants' industrious efforts. Old Faustin and his two sons only spaded the ground in their spare moments; excursions through the woods along the banks of the Red River to those of the Sabine, and hunting and fishing, occupied all their time. They did not dream in the least of becoming rich, but rather of enjoying an independent existence. The petits blancs of the French race, spread throughout America from the St. Lawrence to Texas, have always sought to find a way of making a living while working as little as possible. These men, proud of their white color, reject disdainfully anything that could, to a certain degree, liken them to Negroes. On the other hand, they have lost none of their taste for pleasure and noisy games. Nowhere has the tradition of this joyous life in the woods been preserved more vividly than Upper Louisiana. Several leagues from the Canadians' house, a dozen shacks randomly scattered throughout the clearings formed the center of a little colony that was very poor yet very carefree, and consequently very happy. Étienne, the younger of the two Canadians, went there often, and, as he knew how to draw from a violin several notes that sounded like melodies of *contredanses,* he quickly became the hero and soul of all the parties. His instrument, which an old dancing master from Montreal had bequeathed to him, was hardly a Stradivarius, but a pocket violin good at the very most for making the half-civilized Indians of southern Canada jump. Whenever Étienne passed the bow over the strings of his little violin, not a Creole existed who could resist abandoning his labors or interrupting his nap to run after him.

These pleasures were not at all to Antoine's taste; it was life in the woods that fascinated him. To the great astonishment of the young girls of the neighborhood, he hardly ever left the forest to join in their frolics.

Some of them found him haughty and surly, and others maintained that he was jealous of his brother's successes.

"Son," his father sometimes said, "you are wrong to act like a savage. When the time comes for you to marry, you will be sorry. Look at Étienne—all the women adore him!"

Antoine did not respond and kept on hunting.

Some time after settling in the forest, the three Canadians needed to go to the village to renew their supplies. The night before their departure, Antoine killed a buck and placed it in the pirogue. "This will be for the planter and his daughter," he said aloud as he wrapped the animal in palmetto leaves. "They welcomed us so kindly when we arrived, and we cannot pass by their house without thanking them for that."

"Good idea, my boy," the old man replied. "Ah! These are good people, generous and ready to oblige. In the old days that was the way people received travelers all along the rivers, but today, one finds Yankees [Anglo Americans] everywhere, and they give nothing for nothing, not even a glass of water!"

As they moored their pirogue in front of the planter's house, Marie, who had seen them from afar, came to meet them. Seeing the tall Canadian who approached gravely, walking at a solemn and measured pace with his buck on his shoulders, she felt like laughing.

"Oh! Gracious, Mr. Antoine," she cried out, "what are you carrying there?"

"A bit of small game I killed for you," the hunter replied.

"For us?" the young girl answered. "My father will be delighted with your thoughtfulness. It is very kind of you to have thought of him . . . but wait a moment while I call a Negro. I don't want you to carry that burden all the way to the house."

The Negro hurried so slowly that Antoine had placed the buck on the table before he arrived, and the three Canadians remembered that they needed to set out once again. They had agreed among themselves not to accept the planter's hospitality this time; for their pride's sake, they insisted on proving that this visit was completely unselfish. The planter, after insisting that they stay until the following day, let them go. When they were about to set off, he said to the old man, "Père Faustin, you are making too much of a fuss with an old friend. Of course you promised me that you would stop here on your return, but I don't believe you and I need a hostage. I am keeping your older son. The passenger pigeons that come from the north are beginning to swoop down around the clearings, and the ducks are plentiful on the lakes. Antoine is a good shot. I want to open the winter hunting with him. So go on and leave him with me."

"Agreed," Old Faustin said as he pushed his pirogue off with the gaffe, which propelled it to the middle of the river. Antoine looked around quickly like a bird caught in a trap, then brought his gaze back to the skiff, about to disappear behind an island.

"Well," Marie said, "now you are our prisoner, Mr. Antoine. The pirogue is well and truly gone, believe me. Come have your share of the dinner that awaits us."

Early the next morning, the planter was up and about, his gun under his arm; Antoine, decked out as a scout, wearing a full powder horn on a chain, buckskin gaiters, and a short grey flannel smock, waited for him in the courtyard. They were getting under way and were already marking the route of the expedition when Marie, mounted on a pretty little black horse of Mexican breed, came at a gallop to join them.

"Hey, Father!" she cried. "Wait for me! I want to go along. Go where you wish, and I'll follow you."

"In that case, good-bye to the hunt," Antoine murmured, leaning on his rifle, which came up to his chin.

"Am I bothering you, Mr. Antoine?" the young girl asked.

"I didn't say that," the big Canadian answered. "We will take a ride around the cotton fields, on the beaten paths. It may well be that we'll meet some hummingbirds and some sparrows . . ."

"Marie," the settler interrupted, "how could you follow us in the thickets where we are going? You'll snag your veil on the brambles in the under-brush, you will tear up your hands and face on the acacia thorns. Your horse will end up being frightened by gunshots and will bolt. Come on, be reasonable . . . stay here . . ."

"Fine! Hunt then, sirs, hunt if you wish," Marie replied, giving a flick of her riding crop to her pony. "At least you will permit me to gallop in the woods for a while, won't you, Father?" And she disappeared into the foliage.

Autumn was drawing to an end; the October rains had filled the lakes and ponds. New shoots covered the lianas that had been withered by the scorching summer sun, and they entwined the gnarled trunks of the large trees ever more tightly. Through the dry leaves strewn across the paths, long green grass pushed up from the earth and waved gently in the breeze. The maples had taken on the crimson color of late autumn, and, under the first rays of the day, their dense branches shone like blades of red copper. No cloud altered the deep azure of the sky. It was a second springtime, less cheerful, less flowery, more melancholy than the first. The alligators, about to fall asleep from the torpor into which they sink during winter, came to the surface of the ponds to breathe the mild air of the last fine days. On the dead branches that floated haphazardly and on the knees of the cypress trees, hundreds of small turtles warmed themselves in the sun, spread out in long lines, their heads stretched out, ready to let themselves drop and dive in at the slightest noise. Large birds of prey, some slow and heavy like buzzards, others slender and light like falcons, grazed the cattails and skimmed the clearings with their wings or passed with the speed of lightning over the top of the woods. Occasionally a muffled murmur would cross the opening, similar to the shiver of a sudden breeze that shakes the leaves; it would be a passing flock of wood pigeons hovering in the air, looking for a place to land. No dangerous beast haunted these solitary places too close to the plantations, at least during the day; and so Marie took off fearlessly in that direction. She galloped boldly, skirting the puddles around the moss-draped cypress trees, huge magnolias, and century-old sycamore trees that formed vaults impenetrable by the sun's rays, following at random the half-erased paths that wound through cool valleys among willows and tulip trees. After several hours of riding, she noticed that the countryside was becoming wilder and decided to retrace her steps. Retracing one's way back through the woods is not an easy thing. Marie wandered for some time, unable to leave the labyrinth of thickets that a short while earlier had seemed so graceful—and that now began to frighten her.

In this quandary, the young girl stopped, anxious and trembling, listening carefully, both wishing to hear some noise and fearing it; then she urged her horse to pick up its pace and soon accelerated to full canter. Gunshots in the distance had just alerted her to the hunters' position. Within several minutes she came to a large lake bordered by thorny bushes and covered with a forest of reeds. Clouds of ducks, arriving from every point on the horizon, swooped down on the water and dived and paddled, flapping their wings. Suddenly, the detonation of a firearm forcing them to rise again, they whirled about in terror above the cattails. The great woods that surrounded the lake was a fatal circle these birds could not resolve to cross, and while they swung from one shore to the other, the two hunters drove them back and forth between them. A large number fell; stopped suddenly in flight, dead or wounded, they gave up, their heads lowered in the floating weeds or suspended in the branches. The tall Canadian, standing knee-deep in water several paces from the shore, loaded and fired relentlessly; he was calm and coldly passionate like an old soldier facing the enemy. There were in his movements a precision and an ease that almost resembled grace. When a bird brought down by his lead folded its wings and rolled to his feet, he looked at it with the disdain of a hunter accustomed to attacking nobler prey. The young Creole stopped behind a bush several paces from him and watched with a curious eye. Sure she had found those she was searching for, Marie caught her breath and tried to get over the emotion she felt. Her heart was beating quickly; she felt that she scarcely had the strength to raise her voice, but the thought that she was alone, next to a stranger, prompted her to make an effort.

"Mr. Antoine," she cried as loudly as she could as she stepped into view, "where is my father?"

"Over there, on the other side of the lake. Don't you hear his little double-barreled shotgun thundering like a firecracker?" Having said this, the Canadian took up his position once again; he spotted a dozen snow geese[27] heading toward him, wings outspread, necks outstretched.

"I lost my way," Marie continued, "and I no longer dare go on alone. For heaven's sake, sir, take me to my father. I'm afraid in this forest and I want to rejoin my father, do you understand? I am tired, very tired, and cannot take a step further if you do not accompany me."

She pushed her horse into the water to make herself better understood by the impassive Canadian, who was still following the flight of the geese with the barrel of his gun. These birds, frightened by the sight of the horse and the young woman who moved into view among the cattails, let out a cry and changed direction. Antoine immediately discharged his gun; he cast a spiteful glance at the lovely game escaping him and approached Marie with these four words only: "This way, let's go!" And he led the way at a rapid pace.

"Wait a bit," Marie said. "Not so fast . . . my head is spinning. . . . Oh! my God! I can't see any more . . . I've lost my reins."

"Get down, mademoiselle," Antoine shouted, helping her. "Sit there, in the shade of this tree. This is nothing more than a passing fainting spell, the effect of fear, of a forced march. . . . And what an idea to have followed us all the way to the edge of this lake!"

Women are always the same: they tremble before a spider and unnecessarily confront real dangers! The forest, like the sea, has abysses where the boldest perish! Saying this to himself and under his breath, the Canadian sprinkled onto the young girl's forehead some drops of water, which revived her slowly. When she began to open her eyes, the hunter continued. "Here, I can't offer you a drink from my gourd, but hold out your arm so I can pour a drop of rum into the cup of your hand. . . . Rum! that makes you grimace, doesn't it? Take it anyway, just wet your temples and your lips."

And mechanically she did what he told her. Surprised and happy to see her so compliant to his advice, the tall Canadian contemplated the young girl solicitously. He was close to her on his knees, his head bare, his long black hair floating on his tanned cheeks. A buck could have passed by fifteen paces away without his noticing, but when Marie's eyes opened to meet his, he sprang up suddenly. "Now, mademoiselle, on your horse, please, and let's go meet your father."

And he took the lead, holding the tired animal's reins since she could not yet manage them herself. They made their way slowly along the shore of the lake. The big Canadian walked on the brambles at a bold pace and pushed aside the lianas with his hands, as if he were tracing himself a path through the wheat and cornflowers.[28] From time to time he turned toward the young Creole, seeking to reassure her with his glance. At that moment, Marie no longer recognized this impetuous wild young man who had made her laugh with his manners and annoyed her with his calm indifference. She felt protected by him; he seemed like a compassionate and respectful guide whom she could follow in full confidence. As soon as they approached the planter, Antoine gave the reins back to the young girl and moved his horse behind hers.

"What, Marie! You here!" the colonist cried when he saw his daughter.

"Father, scold me, I deserve it," Marie replied. "But first thank Mr. Antoine. In order to bring me to you, he left the most beautiful position that a hunter could choose . . ." And while she was telling her father what had just happened, the big Canadian self-consciously cleaned the barrel of his gun in silence.

On the grass at the edge of a spring, the planter, Antoine, and Marie ate a meal all three needed after the fatigue and emotions of the day. When they were ready to get on the road to return to the house, Marie could not keep from throwing her arms around her father's neck and crying with anguish, "Where would I be now, my God, if I hadn't found you?"

"Lost, lost forever!" the planter replied. "It doesn't take long for anyone who gets lost in the woods to become completely disoriented. For a long time he wanders randomly, and hardly moving, he muddles up his own tracks, closing himself up in a maze from which he can no longer escape. Fatigue overwhelms him, his mind gets carried away, despair takes hold of him. . . ."

"And the wolves, and the bears! . . . Oh! my God! I'm afraid here. Let's leave, let's go quickly! How can you love these horrible woods so, Mr. Antoine?"

With these words, Marie got back on her horse. Antoine led the way; hanging from his belt he carried as his trophy of the morning's hunt: some thirty or so ducks of various kinds. Bedecked in this manner, he resembled somewhat the fabulous savages shown in prints of old, dressed in a short full skirt composed of a mass of feathers of all colors. His pace had lost nothing of its usual spring; one felt that walking could not tire a man of his caliber. The planter, by contrast, dragged his leg and followed with difficulty the horse his daughter rode as slowly as possible. "I will never undertake a trip like this again," he said, wiping off his forehead, "without being accompanied by two or three blacks to carry my gun and my hunting gear."

The pirogue did not come by again until the following day. Antoine therefore stayed yet another day at the planter's home. He found this time less long than he had anticipated and did not make too much of a face at the young girl who had, by her rashness and thoughtlessness, compromised the success of his great duck hunt.

IV

The planter liked the frankness and the slightly rough innocence of the big Canadian. He never gave up hope of one day drawing him close to himself and making him a partner. "Antoine is the man I need to manage my plantations," he often said to his daughter. "Around here they treat him as if he were a savage because he has a brusque and impetuous exterior, and I myself find him less difficult to civilize than his brother. That one is a lazy good-for-nothing and an idler who thinks only of amusing himself. Unfortunately, the company of such a guest holds no attraction for a young girl, and I dare not invite him to come see us as often as I would like. It's a shame, my child, for with us he would not take long to soften." Marie replied that the Canadian's presence caused her neither pleasure nor displeasure and that she in no way intended to hinder her father's plans.

Antoine went rather frequently to visit the planter, and the planter, to oblige him to return, always asked him for some fine piece of game, turkey, or buck. For her part, Marie, who loved to vary her outfits, would beg him to bring her starling[29] wings and egret plumes out of which she could create graceful headdresses and ornaments for her ball gowns. So far from France and the latest fashions, Creole girls strove to invent anything that lent originality and splendor to their clothing. The surrounding forests cast no hint of melancholy into their hearts. The planters of Upper Louisiana in no way resembled the sad immigrants whose souls are full of nostalgia for their homeland. Established for several generations on the banks of the Red River, they felt marvelously at home and embraced the wild nature that surrounded them. Happy with a generous and free existence, which lent its greatest charms to the pleasures of the hunt and to excursions into the woods, they cleared the land slowly and moderately. Farming extended its conquests every day, but little by little, in an almost imperceptible manner. Civilization rubbed elbows with barbarism. Several leagues from a house where the luxury and urbanity of old Europe reigned, one could find deep in a clearing a nearly naked Indian, poorly armed, slipping through the brush with a furtive footstep, ashamed of being surprised by civilized man in the mysteries of his savage and vagabond life. One day there would be a ball in one of these enormous mansions built on the banks of the river; the next day the same people who had spent the night dancing would camp beside the lake and sleep on the ground rolled in a woolen cover with only the trunk of a tree under their heads for a pillow. The petit blanc especially pushed this carefree cheerfulness to its highest degree, this exuberant liveliness at the heart of the Creole character. Sandwiched between the more or less educated planter and the ignorant and crude child of the woods, he has some characteristics of these two extremes and resembles one or the other of them, depending on whether he obeys the lights of his intelligence or follows his instincts. Thus, whenever the big Canadian Antoine found himself in the planter's family, influenced by the example of more gentle customs and more polished manners, without knowing it he would again become the honest and calm descendant of the farmers who came from Normandy to settle on the banks of the St. Lawrence. When he retreated to the woods, these sentiments vanished quickly; the solitude and silence that bring terror and dejection into weak hearts, on the contrary, restored in him an energy approaching exhilaration. Proud of his youth and his strength, he walked with his head high; he wanted to dominate this powerful nature, which man's hand had not yet begun to tame.

Scarcely had he returned to his cabin when the big Canadian set out exploring the countryside, scouring the thickets and the shores of the lakes. Above all, the banks of the Sabine offered him excellent reserves of large game. Black bears frequented the boggy lowlands, rendered nearly inaccessible by the floods of this great river; there they found dead trees, rotten on the inside and hollowed out with holes as deep as lairs, in which they could easily spend the cold days of winter. To surprise one of these animals in its den and make it come out by throwing flaming reeds on it with a long pole, and then kill it when it slid down the tree—this was an expedition that could tempt a scout like Antoine. Besides, he noticed that the game was becoming less plentiful around his home; an invisible hand was rapidly decimating the birds and quadrupeds almost at his door. The three Canadians met no one for miles around; scarcely a human footstep left here and there its imprint on the paths, and yet someone was hunting on their land.

"There is an Indian who prowls around here sometimes," Old Faustin said, "but the Indian is like the fox—mustn't look for him near the henhouse."

"I'll find him or I'll lose my name trying!" Antoine replied. "I'll find him before the end of winter, and we'll see which one—him or me—will go pitch his tent elsewhere!"

One day then, Antoine, accompanied by his younger brother, headed toward the Sabine. He had discovered the tracks of a bear of great size, and, since winter had arrived, the animal should have already chosen its shelter. The sun was rising; there was some ice around the little puddles and hoarfrost on the grass. The two brothers plunged as deeply as they could into the swamps, across the rushes and the mud, covering this inextricable maze in great strides, leaping onto the crumbling tree trunks that formed a chain of natural bridges. The tiring excursion led them to a little hillock that rose like an island in the middle of the flooded lands. They approached it with caution, and Étienne, who was leading the way, cocked his gun. Antoine took a step to rejoin his brother; he bent down, got on his knees, crawled on his hands, and made a sign to Étienne not to move. Suddenly, standing up, he announced in a low voice, "Some misfortune has happened here. I see a dead man."

"What color is he?" Étienne asked. "It may be a runaway slave [*un nègre marron*] who came here to die."

"No. There's a wild dog running to hide in the bushes. He's not barking—it's the dog of a savage. Those animals are sneaky like their masters. They don't bark, but they do bite."

The two brothers had arrived close to this human form, which frightened them precisely because of its immobility. As he pushed aside the branches, Étienne noticed at his feet a bottle in which a few drops of rum still remained; he showed it to his brother. "I understand," Antoine said. "This is a stupid savage who came here to hide and drink as much as he likes. He put his bottle to his mouth and drank until he had no strength left. With such a dose, he can really sleep without needing to be rocked."

Étienne unrolled the bearskin in which the Indian had enveloped himself like a shroud. "Well," he said to his brother, "our hunt is over. Let's take this skin. After all, it belongs to us since it came from the beast we were hunting. And it will pay us back for part of the game that this prowler stole from us. Listen how he snores! Poor innocent, go on! After all, we're doing him a favor. The cold will awaken him a few hours earlier. On his chin he has two blue lines that cross. Now I recognize him. He's the one you made take a dive the day we arrived in the village. I would bet that his dog recognized us and that that is why he ran away."

While they were talking, Étienne took the legs of the Indian and Antoine lifted him by the head, and they took away the pelt that was sheltering him. "Now," the younger brother continued, "we must give his ammunition a drink. His bottle still contains a good glass of rum. I'm going to pour it into his powder—that'll give it strength."

"And me, I'll spike the gun," Antoine said.

He took the savage's gun, drove a strong honey locust thorn into the *sight*, and broke it off so that it would be impossible to remove. With this done, the two hunters set out on the road home, truly persuaded that after such a lesson the Indian would go far from their neighborhood. When they returned home, they gave the bearskin to their father and thought no more about the encounter.

Several days later, Étienne, wearing his best shoes, his grey felt hat cocked jauntily on his head and a jacket under his arm, walked hastily toward the plantations. His father and Antoine accompanied him. At some distance from their home people were celebrating a wedding to which the whole region was invited. The newlyweds, counting almost as many cousins as there were inhabitants for twenty miles around, had issued a general invitation. Rich planters and petits blancs alike were arriving from every direction, some on foot, some on horseback, others by boat. What happy talk was exchanged on the way! With what enthusiasm people braved the fatigues of a long trip in order to relax by dancing all night and getting back on the road the next morning! Étienne looked forward to a great deal of pleasure at this gathering; he walked so fast that Old Faustin had trouble keeping up with him. As for Antoine, he lagged behind, wondering if he would get to his destination. This frenzy, these dances, this noisy crowd, all of that frightened him. "Bah!" he said to himself. "No one has ever seen me at such a party. Everyone will stare at me. . . . The planter will be there with his daughter! Will they speak to me in front of all these people, to me, a mere petit blanc? And then, if she does speak to me, what will I say back to her? Étienne is truly happy, he is, knowing how to dance and sing and being so bold!"

As he was thinking this way and slowing his pace, ready to make an about-face, Marie, who was following the same route, noticed him from afar. Leaving behind her father, who was trotting gently along with several friends mounted on peaceful mules, she spurred her little pony to a gallop and cried out to the big Canadian, "Come on now, Mr. Antoine, faster than that, or you'll arrive at the wedding tomorrow!"

"Neither tomorrow nor today," Antoine replied. "Having thought it over, I'm not going. What would I do there?"

"But whatever the others do!"

"No, no," Antoine said, shaking his head, "people would point at me. They'd say, 'There's the big Canadian who never comes to our parties!'"

"Oh well!" Marie said. "That frightens you! And these lovely feathers you brought me, you're not even curious to see how they go with my ball gown?"

"Others enough will admire them," Antoine answered in an undertone.

"Good-bye," Marie said sharply. "I'm wasting my time preaching to you. The neighbors are right to say that you're a savage! And my father, who claims that you are changing before our eyes, that you are becoming civilized! . . . Go away, sir, return to your woods, and when you come back to see us, don't forget to hang crocodile teeth from your ears, fasten necklaces of glass beads around your neck, and tattoo your face."

As she was disappearing at a gallop down the narrow path, Antoine remained in the same place, immobile and confused like a hunter whom a partridge has grazed with its wings. "There she is, all angry," he thought, "and all because I don't want to go into this crowd where I have nothing to do! If I had to take her alone through the woods, to take her all the way to New Mexico, she knows quite well that I wouldn't need to be persuaded. I'd throw myself into the fire to save her and her father, too. There's no doubt she'll be lovely in her ball gown, but less so than she was at the edge of the lake when she said to her father, 'Scold me, but first thank Mr. Antoine. . . .'"

The memory of this incident returned more vividly to the heart of the big Canadian, dazed by the reproaches of the same young woman; so he walked on straight ahead. Night fell, he drew near the place of the party, and the noises of the dance wafted to his ears, blended with the rippling of the breeze in the tops of the trees. This feast of Gamache[30] set thirty or so blacks into motion: some, busy with the preparations for the feast, turned spits at the rear of the courtyard; others tied the guests' horses to nearby trees. Several Indians squatting around kettles—lying in wait, along with their dogs, for the leftovers from the meal—filled the role of beggars and gypsies. The windows of the house remained open, for despite the coolness of the evening, the multitude that crowded together in the rooms would have wanted for air.

Pressed behind a tree, Antoine considered this lively spectacle, this rejoicing in which everyone was taking part and which at once attracted and repelled him. Occasionally Marie came to catch her breath at the window; he recognized her among all her companions. Amid the heads that rocked back and forth to the movement of the dance, he always found Marie's; he could distinguish her burst of laughter, the lilt of her voice; but for her, this gathering of graceful young women presented him only a confused blur. When she cast her gaze outside as if to rest her tired eyes from the light, he feared that she would discover him in his hiding place, and he sank deeper into the branches. Most of the evening passed without his being able to do anything but wander around the wedding party. The old people had not stopped smoking under the gallery, letting the young people dance and laugh. When the old ones began to bridle

Théodore Pavie's aunt, Marianne Prudhomme Pavie, had numerous relatives on Ile Brevelle. It is likely that he hunted with them and took his inspiration for the Canadians' hiding place from this scene sketched two decades before writing "La Peau d'ours." *Sketch by Théodore Pavie, 1829–30. Courtesy Chasle Pavie Collection*

their horses to return home, the big Canadian moved away quickly like a night bird that fears being overtaken by daybreak. One of the Indians bivouacking in the courtyard, upon seeing him pass, rested his head on his two hands, stared at him, and emitted a strange laugh that resembled the hissing of a wild cat.

V

Six months later, at the beginning of the summer, the three Canadians went to the village. This time the planter was not waiting for them on the bank of the river, ready to stop them as they went by; violent fevers had spread throughout the region in the spring, and he had emigrated to the highlands with his daughter. Many families had gone, following their path, to settle in the woods and escape the malignant effects that ravaged the plantations. The heat was oppressive; the Canadians rowed as close as possible to the shore in order to stay in the shade of the great trees.

Once they arrived in the village, they moored their *voiture*—as boats were called in that region where no route other than the rivers was known—and busied themselves with sorting out their business as quickly as possible. They were eager to return to their cabin, but how could they leave the shops full of everything—mirrors and powder, boots and violin strings, silks and buffalo pelts, glass beads and hats—where unlimited grog is poured, where they place a box of excellent cigars in front of the buyer, inviting him to help himself to the contents? And then one had to chat with one's neighbors; even competitors came to take part in the conversation and refreshments. The sun was going down and the Canadians had not yet concluded any deals, and they no longer knew exactly what it was they had come to buy.

Antoine said little, as such outings did not amuse him for very long. He was urging his father to leave when a swirl of dust that rose on the horizon and the loud noise of carriages attracted the attention of the village's inhabitants. People came out of the saloons and shops to see the convoy from Mexico pass; the panting oxen pulled with a slow and tired pace the heavy wagons, which soon lined up along the river. While the trail boss looked for a favorable spot to unload his bales of cotton and bundles of pelts, the dealers, impatient to begin bargaining with him, surrounded him, doing a thousand small favors. The herdsmen—hirelings, as they were called, after an old word borrowed from the filibusters—leaned with one hand on their long prods and the other on the horns of their cattle, and they waited for someone to give them the signal to unhitch. These were large, leathery men with complexions the color of dust. They dressed from head to toe in buckskin. They spoke Spanish slightly, English badly, French very badly, and the language of the savages perfectly, but this did not prevent the Creoles from understanding them. One quickly learned from them that the Comanches, the most dreaded of the Prairie Indians, had extended their incursions into the Texas plains between Nacogdoches and Santa Fe, and they seemed to want to push their advance as far as the Sabine.

Since the border was rather poorly guarded on the side of the Mexican provinces, this news caused a certain worry among the settlers. The young people laughed at these fears, which they treated as fanciful; the old people, recalling old memories, were inclined to believe that the Indians would come to "hand it to them," as they said in their primitive language.[31] Although his sons were not in the least moved by this rumor,

Old Faustin shared the opinion of the people his own age, and he left in a state of agitation made rather alarming by the symptoms of fever. Nevertheless, little by little the sight of the woods gave him back his usual serenity and, when he re-entered his cabin, he could not help crying out as he cast satisfied glances around him, "Oh! My boys, we are well off here!"

Several days passed without any confirmation of the news brought by the Mexicans. Then suddenly one morning, the village's inhabitants were awakened from their peaceful sleep by noisy gunfire. In an instant the militia mustered, fully armed, under the command of its officers, and made ready to meet the enemy. The alarm spread quickly throughout the entire parish; people ran from one house to another to warn their neighbors. Everyone sought to flee. Some said they should retreat into the higher lands, and others suggested going down to the village to help the threatened inhabitants. Each planter feared an uprising among his blacks; each petit blanc already saw his corn plants torn up and his tobacco plants trampled underfoot; the ill, and there were a great many of them, begged with wails and tears that they not be abandoned to the fury of the savages. The cause of this panic was the arrival of a horde of Indians who had come to negotiate the sale of their lands with a diplomat called an Indian agent. This agent had as his mission the annual distribution of the somewhat petty presents the government sent from Washington to the chiefs of the neighboring tribes. This was by no means the purple cloth demanded by those barbarians repressed on all points, but measly wool blankets and some trinkets. This time it was a matter of preparing the act of transfer of their territory, and, on this solemn occasion, they presented themselves in great numbers decked out in the most extravagant manner. With the gunshots that had alarmed the population, they wished to convey their power. This *fantasia*,[32] accompanied by fierce howls of a hundred or so warriors covered with animal skins and adorned with floating feathers, resembled an attack far more than the prologue to a peace treaty. Anyone who has seen the spectacle of one of these grotesque victory processions, where hatchets, knives, and spears gleam in the sun, and where scalps of the conquered serve as trophies, will easily understand that an Indian armed for battle and emerging from the forest is a bogeyman capable of frightening not only children but also full-grown men.

To be prepared for any eventuality, the militiamen remained armed, and no one set out into the countryside to reassure the frightened set-tlers. At the first alarm, Old Faustin, whose courage had been altered by a relapse of fever, had taken flight and compelled his sons to follow him. Seeing their father ill and tormented by a vague terror, they obeyed his orders without wondering if his fears were justified. They threw over him the bearskin they had brought back from their excursion to the marshes of the Sabine, closed up the cabin, and left with him. The old man walked, leaning on Étienne's shoulder; Antoine went ahead as scout. When they had been on the run into the forest for an hour, the elder son said, "My father, retreat to the little island in the Red River which faces the place where we hide our pirogue. No one will find you there." The old man nodded, for he was out of breath and could not reply. Finally, as they approached the river, Antoine begged his father to allow him to go to the planter's home or at least inquire at the first houses what had become of him. "Two strokes of the oars," he added, "will put you out of any danger. Our friend is far from his plantation, alone with his daughter in the middle of the woods. If something happened to him. . . ."

The big Canadian had barely taken a few steps away from the river when he thought he heard a sinister howl. He stopped to listen. The same cry rang out again. Rifle in hand, he slipped into a thicket and took off running in the direction of the spot where he had left the old man; then he remembered that the pirogue would have already left his father, along with his brother, on the small island where no one ever went ashore. After running a long distance, he arrived at the summer home of the planter, who was preparing to return to his cotton fields. Marie, already recovered from a temporary fright, had regained her cheerfulness and wits. She joked about the anxieties the big Canadian still felt, and to reassure him completely she read him a letter in which a friend of her father told them everything that had happened in the village.

"I don't know if everything is calm below the river," Antoine replied, "but I am sure I heard the cry of a savage this morning."

"Or a startled owl," the young girl answered. "You have made up your mind to be afraid, and you'll stick to that story for a week. Meanwhile, come with us to the house, and in the future, when there is a wedding in the region, don't let me find you on the roads wandering like a ghost. My goodness! How grumpy you were that night! But I forgive you, because in hurrying to us today you have proved your good heart. Come on, let's go!"

"Mademoiselle," Antoine said gravely, "you're safe here, you and your father. My own father is in danger—at least I believe he is. And he is ill. I must go."

The planter held out his hand to him, and Antoine went away, promising to return to the house soon with news of Old Faustin. Moving at a swift but careful pace, Antoine first ran to the place where he had left his father. It was nighttime; an absolute silence reigned in the forest. No one answered the signal that the Canadian gave those on the island as he advanced toward the water's edge. Surprised and concerned, he looked for the pirogue among the rushes but did not find it. Perhaps Étienne had taken his father back to the cabin. Antoine went there as quickly as he could; weariness weighed him down, but he wanted at any price to clear up this mystery, which was beginning to terrify him. The cabin had been ravaged by fire; it was no more than a heap of charred beams. At the sight of this disaster, the big Canadian, prey to mortal anguish, fell to his knees and began to cry like a baby. What had become of those whom he sought? Were they still alive? To strike out alone through the woods that harbored an invisible enemy would be to hurry to a useless and certain death. It seemed wiser to return to the planter's side and ask him for help.

When he appeared on the threshold, in a state of collapse from this forced march and dying of hunger, worry, and fatigue, Marie nearly fainted. The planter was bowled over at the sight of this big man, haggard and frantic, his face bathed in tears. Without being able to explain the disappearance of the two Canadians, the colonist and his daughter understood that a great misfortune had happened. Instead of squandering vague consolations on Antoine, the planter induced him to restore his strength by taking a little food and resting for a few minutes. "In three hours," he said to him, "we shall be on horseback, you and I. Four trustworthy blacks will accompany us, and, God willing, we shall find those who are missing."

As soon as dawn appeared they were afoot. First they turned their search toward the vicinity of the destroyed cabin. The people they met on the way or questioned at their houses had seen nothing, heard nothing. The savages, they assured them, had not shown themselves there any more than elsewhere; there was not a woman or child who had not recovered from the panic of the preceding days.

"Nevertheless, I heard howls," Antoine repeated. "They burned our cabin down. Ah! The savages, the savages! They have slaughtered my father!"

And as they listened, each one said to himself, "The big Canadian has gone mad!"

While Antoine, the planter, and the blacks accompanying them got under way to scour the wood, Old Faustin and his young son Étienne had already been running without knowing where for more than twenty-four hours, pursued by the sinister yelps that Indians hurl into the air as a death threat. Not finding their pirogue in its usual place, the two fugitives hurriedly left the Red River, from whose banks they did not stop hearing this relentless voice to the right, to the left, and especially behind them. Struck by mortal fear, they wandered through the underbrush without having time to recognize their route. It seemed that a bitter enemy on their trail pushed them forward as the wind pushes a dead leaf. Faustin, devoured by fever, shivered under his heavy bearskin. Étienne supported his faltering father, and they walked without daring to stop for breath. Like an old stag at bay that comes out of a pool of water and can no longer wield his stiffened legs, the old man tottered and collided with the roots of trees; Étienne, tormented by hunger, did not even perceive through the branches the wild fruits that the sun was ripening within reach of his hand.

"My boy," Old Faustin said in a faint voice, "do you see them?"

"No, Father, but I still hear them."

"There are many of them, aren't there? Oh! If only Antoine were with us, we could lean against the trees and hold our ground."

"Oh! Yes, my father, there are many of them. Everywhere we go, their cries ring out. They are spread throughout the forest and they hunt down those who run for safety like us."

Then they looked at each other without speaking, each frightened to see the other in such a state of despair. It did not occur to them that they could expect help from the direction of the habitations, which they believed to have been attacked and pillaged. Nonetheless they had not been forgotten. At that very moment Antoine, accompanied by the planter, was making superhuman efforts to find some clue to their hiding place. Nothing discouraged him. When he saw that the nearest neighbors did not understand the questions he was asking them, he resolved to pursue his investigations. He begged the planter to help him reconnoiter as far as the banks of the Sabine; a vague hope remained in him that Étienne had been able to seek asylum in the same place where, several months before, they had discovered the sleeping Indian. Difficulties with the trail made the journey long and hard; at the mouth of the marsh they had to dismount and entrust the horses to the Negroes. Antoine tried to find their tracks; he jumped from right to left, examining the rushes, probing the moving slime. Suddenly he stopped. "Hear that?" he said in a low voice to the planter, who was following him.

The planter listened. "It's the cry of an Indian," he said. "Let's go get the blacks."

The howl still resounded, shrill like the hideous clamor of the jackal. "Over here!" Antoine yelled. "Let's go, let's go, they're in front of us. I've got their trail. . . . Follow me. . . . Oh! My poor father!"

They quickly approached the place of the funereal cry, which now reached them more distinctly. The moment Antoine prepared to fire on the enemy, whom he judged to be within range, the voice hushed and they heard under the leaves a noise like that of a bird taking flight. The big Canadian tiptoed toward the little hillock. His rifle fell from his hands; he rushed forth like an insane man onto the ground where a man lay in a state of complete immobility. This time the man he found there had ceased living, and this man was his father. A little farther on, Étienne, stretched out on the ground, clung to the roots with his feeble hands and sought to huddle up under the undergrowth like a wounded hare that wants to die out of the hunter's sight. He was barely breathing; his haggard eyes went with terror to his brother, whom he did not recognize.

"It's me," Antoine said as he brought his mouth near the dying man's ear. "It's me. . . . Don't be afraid! Where are they?"

"Over there," Étienne replied, stretching out his hand. "Over there, everywhere! Our father died of fatigue, hunger, and fear. I cannot go on!" And he gripped his brother's wiry arm with what remained of his strength.

"You're not wounded, Étienne! They didn't fire?"

"No, no. I brought my rifle and Father's. . . . They're there, under the grass. . . . I saw only one of them, only one . . . the one who . . . you know, Antoine? He came a little while ago, but I couldn't move! He pushed Father away with his foot, Antoine, and he took back his bearskin!"

The young Canadian survived this catastrophe by only a few days. He died believing that Indians had invaded the region, and, until his last gasp, he thought he heard this terrible voice which, for more than thirty-six hours, had cast incessant terror into the old man's heart and his own. Thus succumbed the old rower and his second son, victims of a ruse that fear kept them from suspecting. After burying his father and watching his brother expire in his arms, Antoine came to seek refuge with the planter. His cabin had been destroyed, and the woods he used to roam with happiness brought back overly cruel memories. He seemed to have given up hunting, and he walked all day within the confines of the plantations, dressed in his Sunday clothing and wearing his grey felt hat encircled by a big black crepe band. For a month, he remained thus in inaction; Marie and her father, respecting the grief of their guest, spoke to him only when he appeared to want them to. What did he plan to do? No one knew.

"My friend," the planter finally said to him, "when you arrived in this country I offered you a house on my lands. Sad events have proven that my advice could have been good! Here you are alone in the world. Stay here."

The big Canadian shook his head.

"And where will you go?" the planter asked.

"That way," Antoine answered, pointing to the west. "That way! I need the woods, sir. I would die here!"

"You will not leave us," interrupted Marie. "My father loves you too much. It would be ungrateful of you."

The big Canadian lowered his eyes, dried a tear, and looked at the young girl with an inexpressible tenderness; then, lifting his head, he said, "I must find him." He began again in a changed voice. "I must find him. I must avenge them!" And Antoine disappeared. No one has ever again heard tell of him.

Today the clearings extend from the shores of the Red River to those of the Sabine, but the cabin once inhabited by the three Canadians has never been rebuilt. The trees they planted have grown with a surprising rapidity and form a cool copse where the chinaberry, wild cherry, and pawpaw trees[33] let their flowers hang among the vines. I camped one evening in this little enclosure transformed into a savannah; it is there that I heard this story from the mouth of an old Creole, a turtle hunter. While he told it to me, the mockingbird, this bird with the flexible and stirring voice who goes looking for a completely solitary man to charm and distract, did not stop fluttering about us; he beat his wings and seemed to regale us with his sweet song, as though we were the guests of this poor cabin so long abandoned.

El Cachupin

EDITOR'S NOTES

This story takes place in the former Neutral Ground east of the Sabine River in the late winter and early spring of 1830. Louisiana had full statehood by 1830, but because the United States relinquished its claims to Texas in the Adams-Onís Treaty of 1819–21, Texas remained under Mexican rule. The diverse ethnic composition of the region predates the surge of English-speaking colonists responsible for the Americanization of Louisiana and Texas. Instead of Anglo Americans, whom he describes as "passionate for adventure and thirsty for conquest," Pavie's characters are Spanish, Mexican, British (Welsh), and African American. All have been involuntarily displaced from their homelands to the Sabine Borderlands.

After the civil war leading to Mexican independence from Spain in 1821, the Plan of Iguala gave Spaniards one year to leave Mexico. Most left, but a few remained, primarily those with Creole spouses. Eight years later, in July, 1829, Ferdinand VII sent General Isidro Barradas with three thousand royalist troops to reconquer Mexico. They were quickly defeated by Mexican troops and tropical diseases, and the Spanish invaders surrendered to Santa Anna in September.[1] Their defeat finalized the expulsion of the Spaniards, including men like Pavie's character Pepo, who had married Creoles and established businesses.

Laffite's pirate band, known as the Baratarians, operated out of a blacksmith's shop in New Orleans and the nearby marshes of Barataria between 1809 and 1814. In 1817 they reestablished themselves in Galveston. John Hopwell, the principal character in the story, confesses to "going to war with his countrymen," probably a reference to the fact that Laffite and his men supported Andrew Jackson's campaign against British troops in the Battle of New Orleans on January 6, 1815. (Pavie notes this fact in *Souvenirs atlantiques.*) For many years after their heroic deeds, however, ships under Jean Laffite and his brother Pierre terrorized cargo ships in the Gulf of Mexico. After the establishment in Galveston was broken up by the American military in 1821, some of Laffite's men chose to settle in the Sabine Borderlands.

GROUPS REPRESENTED
BY THE CHARACTERS

Representatives of four ethnic groups interact in this tragedy, in which Pavie describes the fate of two displaced male aristocrats and two uneducated women. The Spaniard called Pepo had been successfully established in Texas only to be chased across the Sabine by increasing political hostilities in Mexico. This gentleman's economic and political profile is well defined and probably reflects Pavie's empathy for the plight of the Spaniards he encountered in 1829–30. Pepo is accompanied by his Creole wife, Jacinta, whose father, a shipowner and captain, was murdered by pirates in the Gulf of Mexico. Pavie conflates Spanish and French Creole women into a single figure in Jacinta.

As the story opens, an aged, African American couple ferries Pepo and Jacinta from Mexican Texas to the American side of the river, presumably at Gaines's Crossing.[2] The old slave couple has chosen to remain in their shack on the Louisiana side of the Sabine instead of escaping to Mexico, where slavery is forbidden by the constitution. A lonely planter discovers the Hispanic couple resting under a tree and invites them to his tobacco plantation fifteen leagues west of Natchitoches; there, his mixed-race concubine, Cora, becomes both the villain and the victim of the story. Cora embodies the misfortune of uneducated women, one of Pavie's literary themes and real-life causes.[3] The planter Hopwell purchased Cora in New Orleans at a slave auction when she was fifteen, and this implies that neither Cora nor Hopwell are established socially in New Orleans; otherwise, Hopwell would have met his companion at a Quadroon Ball.

Many of the details about Cora's owner and lover Hopwell, a slave-trading privateer turned pirate,[4] suggest that he formerly belonged to Laffite's group. Hopwell reveals his involvement in gambling and African slave trading; he has "lived with thieves for ten years" and is unable to return home to Wales. The model for Hopwell is likely a wealthy follower of Laffite who settled in the Neutral Ground just before Spanish ratification of the Adams-Onís Treaty in 1821 and established a tobacco plantation.[5] Yet he is typical of the Britons Pavie met around the globe who, although used to living abroad, "remained unchanged in the many diverse climes of his travels."

Early in the story, the aristocratic, old ways of Hopwell transcend the immediate situation. In the wilderness, the conduct of the planter, a former nobleman reduced to privateering and piracy, is comprehended by his guests, who share his ancient codes of aristocratic hospitality. But no country remains to support the exiles' comportment, so well practiced in the wilderness by these remnants of a vanished society. Anachronistically, Hopwell consumes dark porter ale in the Borderlands—a small symbol of his homeland. Tethered to a plantation at the opening of the story, Hopwell decides to divest himself of his American wealth and venture to Western Australia, a colony founded in 1829.

As in most of Pavie's stories, the characters' names and head adornments belie their ethnic origins—Jacinta in her veil and tortoiseshell comb, Cora in her white muslin kerchief, Hopwell in his planter's hat, and Pepo crowned with a silk kerchief and sombrero. In these material details, Pavie creates icons of the diverse cultures that enriched the land west of Natchitoches.

BIOGRAPHICAL ELEMENTS

"El Cachupin" illustrates the lesson the youthful Pavie learned in his early travels in pursuit of the happiness described by Rousseau and Chateaubriand: "solitude is worthless for someone who cannot find peace within his own heart." This story demonstrates that no background can ensure happiness, or even safety, in a time of international upheaval, especially among refugees in the former Neutral Ground. Although each character once enjoyed a modicum of stability regardless of life choices, the political and social units in which they thrived have disintegrated. Even when they are physically separated from political threats, the characters fall prey to their inner fears.

Jacinta's fragility and devotion to her husband resemble that of Creole aunt, Marianne Pavie, who abandoned her homeland in the spring of 1830 to accompany her husband to France. Several details of the planter's activities, particularly his love of hunting, suggest Pavie's Uncle Charles, who was a planter. Like Charles, Hopwell rides every morning, rain or shine. Pepo, "less tormented by the need for activity," sometimes seems to be the young author himself, especially when he stays home smoking and leaning on the windowsill, savoring the sweet pleasures of *far niente*. Just as Pavie reported that his uncle did not understand him, Hopwell does not understand the "more placid demeanor" of Pepo. The planter's home, constructed of wooden boards covered with cypress bark, is probably copied from the Pavie plantation, *Ile aux vâches*, in which case the cottage where Jacinta and Pepo are guests might be the cabin Théodore occupied for six months.

In late October, 1829, when Pavie landed in New Orleans and crossed Louisiana on horseback en route to Natchitoches, he encountered several Spanish refugees in the woods. One of the invasion ships had sunk off the Louisiana coast, spilling penniless refugees in the wilderness. Pavie continued to encounter such exiles throughout the winter and spring. They were fleeing overland through Natchitoches to catch steamers descending the Red River to New Orleans, in hopes of returning to Cuba or Spain.

In exercising his gift for creating setting, Pavie matches the calendar of the story precisely to his youthful experience and his observations, reinforced by his notes, sketchbooks, and other writings. The story's clock starts in February, 1830, when the fictional ferry crosses the Sabine; this parallels the moment Pavie and his uncle crossed the river. Numerous snippets come directly from *Souvenirs atlantiques,* particularly the passages about the trips between Natchitoches and New Orleans. Pavie has transferred to the female character his own terror of being lost in the forest; he describes this event, which took place July 2, 1829, in his first book.

While Thédore was living in Charles Pavie's household, his uncle decided to return to France and sold one of his Red River plantations to a French cousin. The price was very advantageous and required no down payment. Thus the struggle of divesting oneself of property to escape to another land was not hypothetical for either of the Pavie men.

I

The winter of 1829, which raged in Europe with such intensity, was just as harshly felt in the New World. There, the lakes of Upper Louisiana became covered in ice and snow fell throughout the low marshy region that stretches from the mouth of the Red River to the Sabine, on the vast warm lands where cotton and sugarcane are grown. The magnolias that lined the streams and the palmettos of the savannahs shivered beneath the frost; the blue jay and the mockingbird could be caught up in one's hand, and the roseate spoonbills fled for warmer climes, leaving the shoals of the Mississippi to the herons and geese. Thus, hunting in the forests was marvelous: the game, not very wild under normal circumstances, now seemed to be sunk into a stupor and barely noticed the presence of humans. But, for the traveler who had to cross these large empty spaces on horseback, this unaccustomed chill was the cause of true suffering. When one stops to eat a meal in the middle of the woods, it is painful to sit on frozen ground; the spring water, so pleasant in the summer in its clarity and intense coolness, is but an insipid beverage when it freezes and the snow alters its purity. These observations will doubtless elicit a smile from those tourists who are now easily and effortlessly crossing the immense territory of the Union with the speed of an arrow, but thirty years ago railroads were not even known by name and the southwestern provinces of the United States retained much of their savage and primitive aspect once one strayed but a short distance from the rivers and streams. A deep silence reigned in these vast solitudes, which were crossed only rarely by wagon trains. The passion for adventure and the thirst for conquest that would one day impel the Americans to cross the borders into neighboring territories were only beginning to reveal themselves in subtle signs of things to come. The Sabine, which separates Louisiana and Texas (which has since become one of the states of the American confederation), thus formed the line of demarcation between Mexico and the United States. No bridge linked the two high banks of this rapid river, rolling its muddy waters beneath the somber foliage of the ancient trees. You could cross the Sabine only on a large flat boat—a ferry boat—maneuvered, not without difficulty, by an old black man whose hair was almost white and a black woman who was certainly more than sixty years old.

One February morning in the inclement year we have been discussing, the old black man and his companion were huddled in the depths of their cabin on the American riverbank, holding fast to one another and remaining perfectly still. Shivering and resigned like two wild cats hidden in the trunk of a tree, they closed their eyes and perhaps fell asleep, for an impatient voice had been shouting "O del bote! Ferry boat!" from the other side for fifteen minutes. And the old couple did not move. The unanswered calls were followed by the sound of a gunshot; this time the old black man got up grumbling and his companion followed him. Their feet were cracked and swollen from the cold; there were rough scales on their thick, inflamed hands. They seized the heavy oars of the boat rather grumpily and slowly propelled it toward the Mexican shore. Two voyagers were waiting for them there, a man and a woman dressed in the garb of the Spanish Creoles. The *caballero,* mounted upon a beautiful horse of the prairies, held beneath his arm the gun he had just fired to call the boat. He dressed like a Mexican traveler: silk handkerchief knotted around his head, large straw hat, short embroidered jacket, velvet breeches open at the knee, gaiters of Andalusian leather, and enormous steel spurs; a woolen mantle with broad red stripes was draped over his shoulder. As for the señora, she was so well wrapped in her silk shawl that one could barely distinguish the tortoiseshell comb placed like a crown upon her head. The regular features of her face showed signs of fatigue, and her little fingers, tapered and white, let the reins of her mule flutter loosely.

As soon as the boat approached, the horseman nimbly jumped to the ground. He led his companion's mule aboard the ferry and, entrusting her with his horse's reins, helped the old black woman maneuver the oar. The force of the current was pushing the heavy flat boat off course on the dark waters of the Sabine; the horse lowered its muzzle toward the edge to quench its thirst, and the mule nervously pricked up its ears.

"Let's row! Row hard!" the rider said. "My good man, you made me wait quite a long time!"

"It is cold," the old Negro responded, sighing heavily. "I was trying to get some sleep."

"Is there some kind of hostel around here, some village?"

"No," the Negro replied. "The village is quite far. First you will come to the highlands where white men grow corn, and then, toward the Red River, you will find the settlements where they grow cotton."

Having thus spoken, the old black man began to groan even louder and the black woman joined him in chorus. The fact is that these two old people no longer had the strength for the job they had been given, and they would not have survived the efforts for long if the route had been frequented more. Their moans were a pathetic cry for the generosity of their passengers, and this time their cries were heard. Touched by their efforts, the horseman placed in their hands a piece of silver so brilliant that they almost fell to their knees. The black woman helped the señora's mule off the ferry, and the black man, showering the generous stranger with blessings, insisted on holding his stirrup while he climbed back into the saddle.

The terrain the two travelers had just alighted onto was covered in large bald cypress trees from whose black and leafless branches hung bundles of moss like somber veils ten or fifteen feet long.[6] After taking a few steps forward, the rider stopped.

"Jacinta," he said to his companion, "let's leave these low, muddy lands as quickly as possible and climb that little hill over there, where we can get some rest."

The horse, prodded on by the spur, crossed the brush, thick with tall grasses and tangled vines, in a sprightly fashion. The mule also trotted along, avoiding with remarkable instinct the little pools of frozen water and the sharp-pointed cypress knees that covered the earth. After a few minutes the travelers reached drier ground sheltered from the wind by a curtain of spiny shrubs. They dismounted; the horseman tied the two animals to the lower branches of a locust tree and spread on the frozen ground the woolen blanket that protected his shoulders from the cold on night journeys.

"Sit down here, Jacinta," he said to his companion. "Aren't you cold? Let me wrap your little feet in the folds of this blanket. . . . Why aren't you answering me? Jacinta! Jacinta!"

Doña Jacinta lowered her head and hid the tears that were streaming from her eyes.

"My poor friend," the horseman said, "exile is hard to take! In the name of independence, in the name of freedom, the Creoles of Mexico have inflicted this upon me. They could not tolerate the presence of a Cachupin[7] among them who remains faithful to his own homeland. Fine! Viva España! They will never elicit from me a single cry, nor a single tear."

Speaking thus, the cavalier stood up proudly and began to roll a cigarette between his fingers. Suddenly, a ray of sun, piercing the haze, flowed through the darkened forest; large birds of prey soared toward the heavens, crying out sharply as if they had been unexpectedly awakened. Winter seemed to flee before the spring. A sweet warm air instantly brought torpid nature back to life. The young woman, lifting her head, threw off the silk shawl that enveloped her and turned toward the cavalier, her eyes filled with tears.

"Pepo," she said softly, "come here, close to me, don't leave me for a second. . . . You are all I have left in the world. This forest is full of sounds that terrify me."

"Listen, Jacinta, listen to what I am about to tell you," the Cachupin said as he sat next to his companion. "If, in following your husband, you have sacrificed more than you can bear, if you miss your native land, your family, there is still time to turn back—the Sabine is there."

"Have I said that I regret my decision?" doña Jacinta replied. "Have you heard a single cry, a single complaint?"

"No, but this obstinate silence, these tears that stream from your eyes betray your sorrow."

"I am suffering," the young woman said. "I am cold and overwhelmed with fatigue. But I want to endure these miseries with you and for you, Pepo!"

"Look, Jacinta, look before you. There, through this mass of trees, what you see is Mexican territory. It is your country, your own homeland—you may never see it again! Your family is there, your friends, the places where you spent the peaceful years of your childhood."

"Yes, I left everything on the other side of this river, I can sense that. I have left everything to follow you, you to whom I am united forever! Pepo, Pepo, give me your hand."

Pepo took his wife's hand. She threw herself sobbing into her husband's arms, and then, lifting her pale face with spirit, she said, "It seems to me that there is no one left on earth but you and me. I like this wilderness now, not a single human creature can be seen, and I am happy here with you. The sacrifice is finished. Where are we going, what will become of us? Only God knows! It is as if a new life is beginning for us. . . . Happy or sad, I accept it, Pepo, and I don't want to cry any more. . . . Look at me. I am gay, happy."

The cavalier tightly hugged his devoted wife, who was trying to smile through her tears. "You are tired, Jacinta," he said. "Rest here for a little while. You will need some strength to continue the journey."

"All right, yes," the young woman said. "I will try to sleep with my head in your lap. I am no longer cold, my friend. The sun is warming me and your affection consoles me."

Wiping her tears, she shut her eyes and was not long in falling into a soft and peaceful sleep, for one good thing about physical exhaustion is that it silences the heart's sorrows. Like a nursemaid who falls asleep rocking a child, the Cachupin was on the verge of falling asleep himself. He tried his best to stay awake, staring ahead at the play of sunbeams on the strange shapes of the tree trunks. In the end, his head fell upon his chest, his eyelids closed, and sleep overtook him.

II

While the Cachupin and his companion slept at the foot of a tree in the middle of the forest, briefly forgetting their sorrows and fatigues, a pair of piercing eyes was fixed upon them. A tall man, with strongly accented features, dressed in the style of an American planter, attentively considered the exiled couple who thought themselves alone in this sad wilderness. He was riding a Creole pony and held beneath his arm a long double-barreled gun; a wild turkey and a half-dozen ducks hanging from his pommel of his saddle were clear indications that he was indulging in the pleasures of the hunt. For nearly a quarter of an hour he remained motionless, hidden behind a thicket, contemplating with an ironic smile the Cachupin who held in his lap the head of his sleeping wife.

"In truth," he said quietly, "here is a charming picture of conjugal love. . . . I am curious to see the woman's face. There are some pretty ones in the Mexican provinces!"

Just as he was saying this to himself, a troop of spotted fawns passed by. The graceful animals leapt over the thickets with the speed of a bird; the sound of their flight, faint as it was, roused the Cachupin from his stupor; he lifted his head and was surprised to see a man on horseback walking toward him.

"Jacinta," he said to his wife, "wake up—we are not alone here."

Doña Jacinta got up immediately, and a blush crept over her cheeks. Suffering and fatigue had given her delicate face an expression of dignity. The stranger approached her with a respect mixed with surprise, greeted her politely, and addressed himself to her husband in Spanish.

"Señor," he said, "when I spotted the two of you from afar, deep in this wild forest, I thought I was seeing Adam and Eve upon their departure from Eden, wandering the deserted earth. Your clothes have already told me what you are, or where you come from. More than one Cachupin has passed through here before you. If you have no shelter, I offer you my own roof. You will be welcome there as fugitives worthy of concern and sympathy. My name is John Hopwell. The land that I cultivate is a few leagues from here, in the highlands."

This cordial invitation, addressed at such an opportune moment, moved don Pepo. "May God bless him who offers us hospitality in a foreign land," he said with strong feeling. "My poor wife is overwhelmed with fatigue, and I accept for her, even more than for myself, your welcoming invitation."

He offered his hand to the hunter, who presented his own, and all three set off at a trot. Doña Jacinta, mounted upon her mule, stayed close to her husband, whose large spurs made a noise like a rattlesnake shaking its tail. John Hopwell's pony, eager to get home, broke into a canter from time to time, but his master's forceful hand controlled him with ease, and he pranced continually, executing graceful bows.

Thus the three of them rode on through the heart of the American forest, each carrying the imprint of the country of his birth. The stern physiognomy of the Cachupin revealed a Castilian type—frank, serious, and proud; on doña Jacinta's gracious face was spread the mysterious charm that is particular to Creole women, a melancholy reflection of the solitudes of the New World. As for the hunter, he had none of the lively and familiar bearing of the Louisiana planters who were of French origin, and he resembled the Yankees established down in the southern provinces even less. Everything in him betrayed a purebred Englishman used to living abroad but unchanged in the many diverse climes of his travels. His energetic gaze seemed to dominate the Cachupin and frighten the young woman a bit, for she didn't dare turn toward him. The three riders barely exchanged words as they trotted through the woods; although they were following the same path, their thoughts wandered in very different directions.

After two hours of travel, don Pepo and doña Jacinta, guided by John Hopwell, arrived at Hopwell's house. The house was constructed of hand-hewn timbers covered with cypress bark. A spacious corridor cut through its entire length. To protect the dwelling from the invasion of reptiles, it was raised about five feet off the ground; a gallery ran around all four sides of the building. It was located in the middle of a large clearing cut into the thick forest, where trees of every species, some dead and despoiled, others full of life and laden with leaves, intertwined their boughs. On the flight of steps leading to the vestibule of this rustic home leaned a dusky complexioned young girl, her bearing careless and nonchalant, and on her head a white muslin kerchief. Her eyes clouded with sadness and anger when doña Jacinta, descending from her mule, leaned upon the hand Hopwell presented to her with a ceremonial politeness.

"Well, Cora," he cried in a booming voice, "how about lunch? Let's go! Let us be served."

The mulatress went to execute her master's orders while he, giving his arm to doña Jacinta, directed don Pepo toward the entrance to the dining room with a sweep of his hand. Some black servants had led the horses and mule away, the voyagers' bags had been placed in a room at the end of the corridor, and Hopwell soon had his guests seated before a generously laid table. Smoked beef, slices of venison, Bordeaux wine—the meal lacked nothing, save perhaps bread, which was replaced by broad thin cakes of corn as yellow as pieces of gold.[8] As they poured the coffee, Hopwell signaled to Cora to leave and addressed the two travelers.

"As we all know, hospitality consists in not impeding the freedom of one's guests. There is on my property, two hundred paces from here, an old residence that I no longer use. It is entirely at your disposal. If it suits you to live there, just say the word and by tonight you will be as comfortably settled in there as one can be in this country."

At first the Cachupin's pride rebelled at the thought of becoming so obligated to a stranger to whom he could offer nothing. This cordial offer only made him feel even more poignantly the miseries of exile. Doña Jacinta seemed troubled and sent her husband a look to encourage him to refuse the proposition.

"We thank you from the bottom of our hearts," the Cachupin replied.

"That means, then, that you accept," Hopwell interrupted with a smile, "and I thank you for it."

"No," don Pepo responded. "We cannot accept your offers, señor Hopwell."

"You are just being polite," Hopwell replied. "Stay here for a few days. The señora needs rest and we, we will hunt. Please follow me, and when you have seen the little house that awaits you, you won't be able to resist ceasing your wandering steps for at least a few days."

The little house, furnished simply but suitably, seemed ready to receive the guests that Hopwell had just brought. Chinaberry trees adorned in their first leaves shaded it on the southern side; leading up to the door was a straight path that disappeared into the depths of the forest. The spot was pervaded by silence, calm, and the tranquil freedom that suits a worried and tired mind. Doña Jacinta let herself drop into a chair and closed her eyes, as if the better to evoke the memory of her father's home, and when she opened them again Hopwell was no longer there.

"What do you want to do, Jacinta?" the Cachupin asked. "Since he wants us to, why don't we stay here a few days?"

"Pepo," she replied, "he is a good and generous man, but despite everything I am afraid of him, and when it is a question of saying no to him, I don't dare. My God! I am so comfortable here! The cold, damp earth can't compare with this old leather armchair—"

"It is true, Jacinta, but we must leave soon, you know! It is always sad to be at someone else's house—"

Thus, as they spoke, the Cachupin and his wife settled into the rustic house. They took possession of it with true pleasure, for they were perfectly free there and quite at home. But while the fugitive couple tasted a tranquil repose beneath this hospitable roof, Cora, the mulatress, watched their movements from afar with jealous concern. When evening arrived, Hopwell began to stroll about the gallery of his home, and as he walked and smoked Cora slid up beside him like a shadow.

"Master," she said softly, "who are those people you have settled in down there?"

"What does it matter to you?" Hopwell replied.

"She is pretty, that woman," Cora said.

"Yes, very pretty. . . ."

"But really, master, why have you lodged them in the old residence?"

"Because I am bored in all this solitude and it suits me to have people near me."

"You are bored! . . . Why did you give up the sea? Why did you sell the schooner?"

"Because I didn't want to be hanged by the neck at the end of a yard-arm," Hopwell answered. "Trading and hunting offer some advantages, but they also have their dangers. You must know when to stop."

"So you met these people in the forest while hunting?"

"The señora was sleeping, overcome with fatigue, her head on her husband's knees. When I saw them I began to smile. Then I took a step toward them and I was touched by compassion. They seemed so miserable but at the same time so happy. I looked at them for a long time— happy people! You don't see that every day!"

"But these foreigners have nowhere to go," Cora said. "It is not they, it is you who are happy, master!"

"Do you think so?" Hopwell said. "Having chests full of gold and living far from the eyes of men, in the heart of the forest, without daring to show oneself in one's own country, do you call that being happy? After having gone to war with my brethren, now I battle game in this wilderness, and then I watch my black slaves plant corn! A wonderful existence, isn't it? For ten years I lived with thieves. Now I live with twenty slaves who are afraid of me. Sometimes it makes me want to give them all their freedom, to run away from here and throw myself into new adventures—"

"And me, master, what would become of me?" Cora asked, clasping her hands.

"You?" Hopwell replied. "I will give you a thousand piasters right now, if you like. Go on. Leave here, make a fate of your own choosing."

"No, no!" the mulatress cried. "I will never leave you! Even if you banish me from here I would never leave! Master, dear master, I beg of you, keep me with you always! What have I done to make you hate me so, all of a sudden?" Cora had thrown herself at her master's knees and was kissing his hands.

"You don't understand me," Hopwell said. "It is for your own good that I say this, and for mine as well. This Cachupin and his wife interest me because they are fugitives, exiled from their homeland, and I am like them. My family cursed me. If I return to Wales, all doors will be closed to me."

"Why would you go back there? Don't you like living here? Oh, dear master, you are sad tonight! Would you like a glass of porter?"

"Leave me, Cora. I need to be alone."

"Or perhaps a glass of the old brandy that made you so proud and brave on the coast of Africa?"

"You are my bad genie, Cora. Go on!" Hopwell said imperiously.

"You are tired of me, aren't you?" the mulatress replied. "The doe eyes of the Espagnolette have turned your head."

Cora, who feared her master's anger, disappeared as she uttered these impertinent words. Remaining alone on the gallery, Hopwell continued to pace back and forth as if he were on the bridge of a boat. Those who have sailed for a long time experience a supreme pleasure in walking thus back and forth in a narrow space. This monotonous promenade plunges the body into a kind of somnambulant trance and one becomes like a sleepwalker, barely aware of what one is doing. One believes himself surrounded by the limitless ocean, one hears the roar of distant waves, one dreams, one remembers, and thoughts fly off into infinity. Hopwell, prey to a profound melancholy, remained like this for a long time, striding up and down the long gallery, from which he could observe the clearing around his habitation. The dark night swallowed up the surrounding landscape in shadows, and although he could see nothing, Hopwell continued to turn his head toward the long-deserted house that now served as asylum for his guests. "There," he thought bitterly, "are two people who love each other, who suffer for each other, who walk through life without remorse or shame. Wandering fugitives such as they are, I am reduced to envying them even though I have more wealth than you would need to heap ten families with joy and happiness. . . . Gold is a funny thing, coveted by those who don't have it but often useless to those who do!"

III

It so happened that it rained for the next several days, during which time the Cachupin and his wife could not think of beginning their journey anew. They led an extremely peaceful existence in their rustic abode. Every morning Hopwell had breakfast taken to them, and in the evening he invited them to dine with him. Under the influence of a more temperate climate, doña Jacinta began bit by bit to recover from the exhaustion of her journey. The last traces of the harsh winter rapidly disappeared, and barely a week after the frosts the buds on the trees were swelling with sap. The songbirds, the cardinal, the mockingbird, and many other winged creatures with gay plumage began to fill the forest with their joyous sounds. All that was missing was the hummingbird, which waited to appear until the flowers began to bloom so that he could once again inhale their heady essences. The caiman was already awakening in the deep waters; the turtle, emerging from his long lethargy, undertook his slow peregrinations through the woods. On the shores of the lakes, the eagles hurried to prepare nests for their broods; swooping rapidly, they carried in their hooked beaks dried boughs and flexible roots that they arranged into nests at the summit of sycamore trees.

Accustomed to an active life, Hopwell went horseback riding every morning, rain or shine. Don Pepo, less tormented by the need for activity, usually remained leaning on the windowsill near doña Jacinta, smoking a cigarette and savoring the sweet pleasure of *far niente*. Physically flying toward the horizons or intellectually summoning them forth in one's mind for contemplation are two equally valid ways of identifying with nature, but Hopwell, who was an energetic man, did not understand the more placid demeanor of his guest.

"Don Pepo," he often said, "would you like me to saddle up your horse?"

"Tomorrow, tomorrow," the Cachupin answered, smiling, and he remained in the same place rolling cigarettes, his sombrero pulled down over his eyes, his large striped mantle flung over his shoulder. One morning, however, he had his horse saddled and left with Hopwell.

"Very good," Hopwell said. "You have finally decided to take a ride in the forest."

"Yes," the Cachupin replied, "because I want to talk to you and in this wilderness we can speak quite freely. We have been staying with you for a long time, Mr. Hopwell."

"A long time! . . . But it has been barely a week."

"Indeed we have been your guests for an entire week. It has stopped raining and the skies are now clear and serene. Jacinta's emotional and physical strength have been restored. It is time now for us to leave you."

"Where will you go?"

"We will go where God wills us," the Cachupin said, sighing.

"Life is sad here, I agree," Hopwell said. "Since I have lived in this wilderness I haven't had a week of happiness."

"My dear host," the Cachupin replied, "hospitality is a great kindness, and I come from a country where we know how to practice this noble virtue, but in the depths of our hearts is a wellspring of pride. In welcoming us into your home, you have done your duty as a caballero, and I must do mine by declaring that it is impossible for us to remain beholden to you any longer."

"All right," Hopwell said. "Let me reverse the question. I am indebted to you, and I am asking you to stay with me a little longer. Chance has tossed me into this wilderness. Like you, I was born in Europe. Youthful blunders and a passion for adventure drove me away. America is rejecting you and Europe is open to you, but I—"

"Alas," the Cachupin said, "I had left for Mexico with the hopes of making a brilliant fortune, but the revolutions decreed otherwise. Once settled in Texas, I built up a sizable commercial establishment and had just married Jacinta. My happiness lacked nothing, and then a series of catastrophes befell me. Jacinta's father was the owner and captain of a commercial brig that sailed the Gulf of Mexico. Returning from New Orleans with a rich cargo, he was attacked by pirates—or some say by Negroes, but it's all the same, isn't it?—and my wife's father, struck by a cannonball on the poop deck of his boat, died before he could see everything he owned pass into the hands of these brigands. . . . Thus perished the *Mariposa*."

"Was that the name of the brig?" Hopwell asked, swatting at the tall grasses with his crop as his horse trampled through them.

"Yes, sir. From that sad day forward she ceased to exist for us, the *Mariposa* that had made the fortune of Jacinta and her father. My business remained and I lost nothing, but then the revolutionaries decided to drive out all those who were Spanish by birth, whom they didn't trust, and I had to leave everything and flee, bringing nothing with me but the last and sovereign good that only death can take from me, the beloved wife who has tied her fate to mine."

"That is enough to be happy," Hopwell said sadly, "and I would trade my fate for yours."

"I was barely able to raise the sum of one hundred ounces of gold before I left," continued the Cachupin. "What will I do with this tiny capital? I still don't know."

"We will talk of this at our leisure," Hopwell responded. "Stay, stay, amigo. Wait for things to take shape and then you can make up your mind."

Thus spoke the two riders as their horses trotted along in the green grass. They went on randomly, following the contours of little lakes over which gigantic trees, half smothered in vines as thick as cables, dangled their heavy branches. By the banks of the streams, huge magnolias with slick gray trunks raised their verdant heads, adorned with large flowers as white as snow, spreading a heady perfume far and wide. The black branches of the cypresses were covered with the tender green leaves, so finely delineated, that signal the return of the warm seasons in this clime. Everywhere the sap was rising, and one could see the foliage thickening from one hour to the next as the knotty trunks disappeared beneath the new buds. Across the boughs the little gray squirrels and the large fox squirrels gamboled and romped as they played, without taking notice of the two riders, whose horses, equally enlivened by the spring air, let out loud whinnies. From time to time the deer, troubled in their repose, rose abruptly and disappeared into the forest, as light as shadows in the deep thickets.

In these vast spaces where nothing marks the distances, it is impossible to go out for a stroll or a ride without covering at least four or five leagues. When they returned to the house, Hopwell and the Cachupin had been gone for at least three hours. Doña Jacinta, who could not be separated from her husband without experiencing a vague disquiet, ran to meet them.

"Mr. Hopwell," she said to the planter, "you have kept my Pepo too long. I will never let him go off with you again!"

"Next time, señora," Hopwell said, moving away, "I will bring both of you and the time will pass more quickly for all of us."

"Well," doña Jacinta said to her husband, "did you talk to him about our leaving? When will we set out again?"

"I spoke, but he avoided answering me. Tonight we will both talk to him about it and ask him for his leave. It would be rude to leave abruptly."

That night at dinner, don Pepo and doña Jacinta told their host of their decision to leave. They wanted to depart early the next morning.

"Wait just a little longer," Hopwell said. "Why hurry? Besides, perhaps I will leave with you. I have a trip to make."

These words were overheard by Cora, who was sitting in the corner of the dining room, her eyes half-closed in silent reverie. She carried a violent hatred for these two strangers whom her master endeavored to keep close to him, and doña Jacinta's presence in the house had become intolerable to her. She could not get used to seeing this woman of a race superior to her own, adorned with all the graces that virtue adds to beauty, seated every day at her master's table. Jealously she noticed that since the strangers' arrival, Hopwell hadn't been himself. This man, whom she had known to be violent and passionate, dominated by bizarre and sometimes savage instincts, had each day become calmer and more serious. The attacks of spleen he was subject to and that he combatted all too often with rum and whisky had given over to attacks of deep melancholy at once gentle and resigned. His thoughts no longer followed their usual course. An unexpected decision was growing in this mind that had been so tormented by storms of passion and perpetually in search of peace. But every change in Hopwell's lifestyle seemed to Cora an irreparable misfortune that would upset her very existence. She trembled at the thought of seeing her master suddenly tear himself away from the peaceful wilderness and its mysterious charms, which she shared with him.

Hopwell's words pierced straight to her heart. Once the Cachupin and his wife had retired, she approached her master, and, restraining her emotion with difficulty, asked, "Master, why won't you let them leave?"

"You will know when it is time for you to know," Hopwell answered.

"So you don't want to tell me anything more? Has poor Cora lost her master's confidence?"

Hopwell paced the length of balcony without responding; he was pale and agitated.

"Ah, dear master," Cora said, "you are unhappy, you are suffering! Since these people arrived, we don't recognize you. It is time for them to leave, for you as well as for me."

An impatient gesture was Hopwell's only response.

"They are settled in as if they lived here," the mulatress continued. "The señora, with all her affectations, comes and goes throughout the plantation as if she were no more or less than the mistress of the place. These people have nothing, not even an inch of land, and they look upon you with the airs of great landowners!"

"Be quiet, Cora," Hopwell said.

"And you are at their beck and call. You, master, you before whom everyone aboard the schooner trembled, you are on your knees before the Cachupin and his wife."

Hopwell stopped and glowered angrily at the mulatress.

"Here, master," she cried, "take your crop and strike me, strike poor Cora—"

Hopwell had seized the crop with haste and held it in the air, and then he slowly lowered it and began to gently swat the dust that covered the bottom of his pants.

"Not a word of response to my questions, not even the blows that I deserve!" Cora said dully. "A dog would be treated better—"

"Cora," Hopwell replied, "go tell my guests that I would like them to have tea with me. I need to speak with them."

"No," Cora said, shaking her head, "no, I will not obey." She cowered in a corner of the balcony and hid her head in her hands. Without another word, Hopwell went himself to find the Cachupin and his wife, and several minutes later he returned, giving his arm to doña Jacinta. That day Hopwell had the solemn gravity of a Quaker and the dignity of a gentleman.

"Don Pepo," he said, "and you, doña Jacinta, listen to the project that I have formulated in my mind. I can speak openly and without fear of being overheard by anyone, for none of my servants is nearby. I must leave these parts, where life is no longer happy for me. I have a past that must be atoned for elsewhere. Later you will know everything, but for today suffice it to say that I am giving you this plantation with all of its lands for whatever price you would like to offer. The blacks and all the servants of the house will become free, and I, free as well to begin my life anew, will pitch my tent in the Australian wilderness. Everywhere is good to one who no longer has a homeland. Here, don Pepo, you won't be far from the country that you have adopted, and where you may be able to return one day. You, señora, you will be able to maintain regular contact with your family. Doesn't the Sabine run quite close to my plantation? Beyond that river lies the country of your birth, the country you could never completely renounce!"

Hopwell's vibrant voice revealed his energetic will. He knew well how to impose what he wanted on others. When it behooved him to suppress the haughty and imperious impulses that came naturally to his character, he still retained the ability to cast a spell over those who approached him, a power that is the product of a spirit strong and sure of itself. As he spoke, the Cachupin lowered his head and listened attentively to his words, and doña Jacinta, troubled to the very bottom of her heart, turned toward her husband with eyes moist with tears. All he wanted was to stop their fugitive flight a few leagues from the border. The uncertainty of the future, the worry about tomorrow that brought more insomnia and anguish than present woes, disappeared for them like ghosts in the night who dissipate with the coming of the dawn. They both felt that surprise that consoles and frightens at the same time, for the human soul cannot pass from sorrow to hope without fearing that it has been duped by some kind of illusion.

Don Pepo and doña Jacinta's silence had all the eloquence of an affirmative reply. Hopwell understood and began to speak again: "Your acquiescence to my proposal overwhelms me with joy. Thanks to heaven, thanks to you, I am going to tear myself away from this life, which is only good for nourishing spleen. Solitude is worthless for someone who cannot find peace within his own heart. In two days' time we'll go to New Orleans together. There, my business manager will conclude in a legal and authentic way the little arrangement that we have just agreed upon."

"May it be so, señor Hopwell," the Cachupin said. And, pulling from his finger a large gold ring, he added, "Please accept, as of today, this little present as a sign of our gratitude."

Hopwell took the ring and examined it closely. On it was a ship, all its sails unfurled, with this legend: *Mariposa, Dios te guarde!*

"Keep this jewel, which brings back such sad, cruel memories," Hopwell said, quickly thrusting back the present don Pepo had offered him. "It is not mine to wear!"

Then, fearing that he had wounded his guest with the brusqueness of his refusal, he added, "Later, when the affair is concluded and the deal is closed, then will be the time for us to exchange presents, the way diplomats do after signing a treaty."

IV

Although the railroads did not yet exist in the United States when these events took place, steamboats had been ploughing through the North American rivers for several years. Great steamers leaving from New Orleans began to sail up the Mississippi, linking the capital of Louisiana to distant towns that were soon to become highly populated centers of considerable importance. The ships that navigated the Red River terminated both summer and winter in the village of Alexandria, for the shallow waters roiling around the rocks formed rapids that were impossible to cross during these seasons; but in the springtime, the river rose as the snows from the Rocky Mountains melted, pouring torrents of yellow, muddy water into the riverbed, and the ships advanced past Alexandria as far as the furthest habitations of the Natchitoches parish. It was to the village of this name, situated fifteen leagues from his home, that John Hopwell drove the Cachupin and doña Jacinta to embark with them on the journey to New Orleans.

When she saw the two strangers preparing to leave, Cora experienced a strong feeling of satisfaction. The somber sadness that had overwhelmed her for the last few days suddenly lifted, and she gave way to transports of mad joy. Hopwell also appeared calmer; the important projects that he was going to execute and that he had not fully revealed to anyone preoc-

Though steamboats could come up the Red River as far as Natchitoches only a few months a year in 1830, barges had been descending the river to deliver merchandise to New Orleans for more than a century. The "village" of Natchitoches and the "city" of New Orleans served as gateways to Texas and the West. *Pierre Marcotte's map, courtesy Cammie G. Henry Research Center, Northwestern State University, Natchitoches, La.*

cupied him. Forgetting a past full of painful memories, he glimpsed with a more peaceful eye the prospect of a regular future. None of the servants who surrounded him suspected the decision he had just made. When he gave the order to saddle his horse, Cora, not remembering the trip he had spoken of two days earlier, imagined that he was simply going to accompany the Cachupin and doña Jacinta for a few leagues to set them on their way.

"Master," she said gaily, "be careful to show them the road they must follow, or they might get lost in the forest and then perhaps they would come back."

"They will not get lost," Hopwell replied. "You can be sure of that, as I am leaving with them. Go find my suitcase."

"Where are you going, master?" Cora asked with surprise. "As far as the village?"

"Further, all the way to the city.[9] I will be back here in two weeks."

This brief reply plunged Cora into new state of unease. What was her master going to do in New Orleans? This abrupt departure was doubtless hiding some mystery. Falling prey to the most melancholy foreboding, she watched the three travelers disappear beneath the large trees of the forest, heaping curses on the Cachupin and his wife and all the while hoping that her master would turn back toward her with some farewell gesture. But Hopwell rode off at a brisk trot without turning his head, and Cora, remaining alone on the gallery of the house, melted into tears. It seemed that all was lost for her. The beautiful spring days, filled with bird songs and warmed by a radiant sun, seemed gloomy and chill now. For someone with a broken heart, nature's smile holds nothing but bitter irony, an insult to his sorrow. This woman, in the habit of giving in to her most violent instincts, and whose uncultivated mind could never rise above material sensation, passed quickly from sadness to anger. She began to trample underfoot the sweet-smelling pawpaw flowers hanging in festoons around the trees and to hurl stones at the little birds chirping in the groves. Left alone with absolutely nothing to do, she spent long hours in her master's parlor. There, before the mirror, she dressed her hair in twenty different ways and coiled crowns of leaves in her thick tresses; then she scattered these useless ornaments and stomped her foot on the ground, irritated to find tears quivering at the edges of her eyelids. She was a poor creature and worthy of pity, a woman who had neither soul nor intelligence but whose heart was overflowing!

As Cora abandoned herself to a hopeless despair on this silent and empty plantation, Hopwell and his traveling companions arrived in New Orleans. The affairs that had brought them there were quickly concluded. Hopwell ceded his entire plantation, with all of its cattle, horses, and equipment—everything except the slaves—by legal deed to don Pepo and doña Jacinta for a modest price calculated on the slender capital that the Cachupin had at his disposal. This sale was almost a gift; however, he who dispersed his wealth without seeming to know its worth experienced as much and even more satisfaction than those to whom he bequeathed his possessions. Finally free to leave this country to which he was no longer tethered, Hopwell was impatient to return to the plantation to set everything in order and take flight to faraway lands. He immediately settled his passage, with don Pepo and doña Jacinta, on a steamer that would take the three of them back. The Mississippi flowed along, filled to the brim by the torrents of spring, its yellow waves lapping at the base of the embankments erected to protect the sugarcane plantations. A few tree trunks, uprooted by the waters, floated in the current like canoes, and ash-colored herons hovered motionless above, sailing along haphazardly with the meditative attitude of these great wading birds. The thawing snows of the Rocky Mountains had also swelled the waters of the Red River, rendering its flow more rapid. Despite its powerful engine, the steamer advanced slowly, sometimes forced to sail close to the banks of the narrow river whose shores were still covered in forests. In many places these river-swept forests took on the appearance of a boggy marsh where one could see, through the dead branches and hanging vines, fat caiman covered in mud warming themselves in the sun and tortoises with dazed expressions plunging into the water only to reappear a little further away. These amphibians seemed to enjoy complete happiness in these warm, muddy waters where they alternately walked and swam, using the double privilege that nature bestowed upon them in compensation for their ugliness.

The steamer had left New Orleans five days earlier and had been traveling up the Red River for twenty-four hours. Some travelers, armed with rifles, amused themselves by shooting at every sort of animal that crossed their path, others played cards, and still others smoked endlessly and made frequent visits to the refreshment room. There were also some passengers who found a way to fill the brief intervals which in America, separate the four meals of the day, with light reflection. Time passed slowly but pleasantly. Hopwell and the Cachupin usually walked on deck, chatting with the familiarity of two friends, while doña Jacinta, seated nonchalantly on a bench, watched whatever passed before her eyes without much attention. In the heart of this young woman, born in the warm provinces of Mexico, there was but one sentiment—devotion to her husband—and the affection that she dedicated to him absorbed her so completely that she seemed indifferent to everything else. It is often thus in countries where the incessant distractions of the world are unknown and where all joy is found in the delights of peaceful conjugal bliss. If doña Jacinta dreamed of anything during the hours she spent sitting on the deck of the steamer, it was of the tranquillity she would enjoy with don Pepo in the deep wilderness that awaited them.

It would take another day for the steamboat to reach the point where it was supposed to deposit its passengers on dry land. In spite of the difficulties of navigation rendered even greater by the rapidity of the current during the torrents, the ship's pilot insisted on sailing at night. The moon shone brightly, slicing through the dark shadows of the big trees and throwing a luminous limpidity on the impetuous waters. The women withdrew to the cabin reserved for them, as did the gentlemen, and only Hopwell and the Cachupin remained on deck. The air was soft and warm, and the Cachupin decided to sleep beneath the stars, wrapped in his woolen shawl, as he had so many times before on his journeys across the deserted plains of Mexico.

"Good night," Hopwell said. "My cigar is finished and I am going to lie down within the four walls of my cabin, by the smoky light of my lamp."

"Buena noche, amigo," the Cachupin responded. "I would rather stay here in the open air, by the light of the moon." He walked a little longer, smoking half a dozen cigarettes, and then he sat down on the edge of the boat, resting his head on his chest. Little by little sleep overtook him; the boat continued to advance, a column of red smoke billowing from its white chimney and pouring a blazing light on the waters. The violence of the current increased in direct proportion to the narrowness of the river, and the tree trunks, sticking up in the middle of the passage on unseen shoals, frequently forced the steamer to hug the shore. In one of these abrupt, unexpected movements the prow was thrown against the riverbank, and without a prompt maneuver of the rudder the steamer would have been thrust into the middle of the half-submerged forest, whose opaque shadows traced the ship's profile. The boat righted itself and took up its straightened course, but as she moved forward a treacherous branch hanging over the waters swept one side of the deck. The Cachupin, struck while asleep, was thrown overboard. He cried out, but the noise of the wheels muffled his voice, and the waves stirred up by the wheels, forming eddies, immediately covered him. Hidden in the shadow of the woods, he was not seen by the pilot, who was inspecting the other side of the boat, lighted by the moon's rays.

Reviving after a momentary stupor, the Cachupin began to swim vigorously toward shore. When he was almost at arm's reach, the muddy soil gave way beneath his feet and he fell back into the current. Ten more times he tried to extract himself from the impetuous billows that seemed intent upon seizing him once again. Now the branch he pulled toward him broke in his hand; now his shriveled fingers sought vainly to grasp the walls of the steep banks of the river; now he became entangled in the inextricable maze of spiny vines. For half an hour he battled the multiple obstacles that rose up before him. In the end he reached a spot where the gently sloping grassy banks presented a port of refuge for a shipwrecked soul like himself. The Cachupin, half-dead with exhaustion, let himself collapse there, and there he remained, stretched out and unconscious, for a period whose duration he would never know. He felt at once like he

Théodore Pavie almost drowned the day before he arrived in Natchitoches in October, 1829. The loneliness of his struggle against natural forces is echoed in the Capuchin's experience and seen in this early pencil sketch. *Sketch by Théodore Pavie, 1829–30. Courtesy Chasle Pavie Collection*

was brought back to life and sleeping the sleep of the dead. The morning's freshening cool woke him from his torpor; soaked to the bone and deprived of his woolen mantle, which the current had whisked away, the Cachupin shivered from head to toe. He rose and began to walk without knowing where he was going. No house presented itself to him, and no path traced by human feet revealed the route he should follow. Here and there in the middle of the woods, small clearings opened up, filled with water and covered with wild ducks that rose into the air and disappeared over the tops of the trees. The wilderness stretched as far as the eye could see, full of charms for one who sought them deliberately on a stroll, but full of terror for someone plunged into its depths without being able to leave them. For several hours the Cachupin wandered aimlessly; fatigue overwhelmed him, and his damp clothes stuck to his skin with an intolerable clamminess. Forced to stop, he sat down in a sunny clearing and listened attentively to the thousand sounds of the forest. Through the cries of the birds and the murmur of the wind, he thought he could make out the sonorous voice of a cock, a sure sign of a human habitation. To understand the emotion that this loud and joyous cry evoked in the abandoned traveler, one must also have suffered hunger and thirst in the wilderness. For the Cachupin this was a friendly voice that told him to gather up his courage; heeding its encouraging message, he began to walk once again with a more confident step. Soon an impoverished-looking house, inhabited by a family of poor white settlers, appeared before him. Fever reigned in this isolated homestead; nevertheless, the settlers cordially welcomed the Cachupin, whose state inspired pity, and extended toward him every sacred duty of the hospitality of yore.

After don Pepo's fall, the steamer had continued on its course, and the passengers, deep asleep, never suspected that an errant tree branch had just swept away one of their companions. When the sun rose on the horizon, Hopwell calmly dressed and went up to the deck. Doña Jacinta soon appeared there as well, and, surprised not to see her husband, asked Hopwell, "Where then is Pepo?"

"I imagine he is still sleeping, señora. It was almost midnight when I left him, and he didn't seem ready to go to sleep yet."

Thus speaking, Hopwell went into the large room and examined one after another of the bunks where some passengers were still resting. The Cachupin's was still empty; Hopwell went back to the deck alone. "I didn't find him, señora. Perhaps he went to light a cigarette in the engine room."

"Jesus!" doña Jacinta cried. "Pepo, Pepo, where are you?"

She began to search everywhere, among the firemen and even in the hold. No voice responded to her call; she saw nothing but surprised and indifferent faces, black, yellow, and white.

"Oh my God," she said suddenly, dropping onto a bench. "Last night I heard a cry, oh! yes, I remember it now, a heart-rending cry, a cry of distress. . . . It was his voice, it was Pepo calling for help! And I went back to sleep, thinking that I was dreaming! Captain, where is the captain? Mr. Hopwell, call him please! We must turn back, we must find my husband!"

The captain had come running at the sound of this desolate voice, which roused everyone on the deck. "Madame," he replied, "if your husband made it to shore, which we have every reason to believe, he did not remain on the banks of the river to wait for us. If he had the misfortune to disappear in the current, we won't be able to find him alive. In a few hours we will reach our destination, and from there you can send someone in search of your husband."

Doña Jacinta stood stock still, her eyes fixed on the man speaking to her, not seeming to understand a word he said. Sorrow knows no reason; stunned by the blow that had just struck her, the Cachupin's wife threw herself at the captain's feet, seized his hands, and cried out in a harrowing voice, "Give me back my husband, Mr. Captain, sir. You are the master here—in the name of heaven, give me back Pepo!"

V

Hopwell knew that he could not leave doña Jacinta alone in her prostrated state. Despite his own ardent desire to search for the Cachupin himself, he had to entrust this mission to one of the Creoles of the village—today the city of Natchitoches—where the steamer had just arrived. The Creole left in a light canoe and quickly descended the Red River. Before nightfall he passed the spot where the Cachupin had been tossed into the water, and soon he discovered the red-striped woolen mantle hooked on a clump of cattails. Collecting the mantle and taking it back to those who had sent him in search of the Cachupin seemed to be the best course of action. Unable to return by water as quickly as he wanted, he left the canoe moored in front of the first habitation he came upon. There they lent him a horse, and after trotting all night, he presented himself to Hopwell first thing the next morning. Doña Jacinta, who anxiously watched for the Creole's return, began sobbing at the sight of the mantle soaked by the river waters.

"Señora," Hopwell said, "you must remember that they brought Joseph's tunic stained with blood to Jacob, and nonetheless this much-lamented son was found again one day."

"My God!" doña Jacinta cried, wringing her hands. "Only you know the anguish I am feeling! Mr. Hopwell, I beg of you, tell me what I should do."

"Send out a new search party of energetic, intelligent people to look for don Pepo and come back to my house as quickly as possible. The discovery of this mantle proves nothing."

"You are trying to fool me, Mr. Hopwell!"

"No, señora, no. Your husband would have thrown it off so he could more easily get to shore."

"Perhaps you are right," doña Jacinta replied, "but I cannot overcome my own fears, nor can I resist the worries that assail me. Let us go, if you please. The sight of this boat overwhelms me with sorrow."

Hopwell and doña Jacinta mounted their horses and left immediately; they went quickly, keeping a profound silence between them and giving themselves over, each on his own side, to all sorts of conjectures. The sun had not yet set when they saw the plantation, which stood out in the middle of its vast clearing surrounded by majestic trees. Cora, who awaited her master's return with a feverish impatience, let out a cry of joy when she heard a horse whinny in the forest. She leapt up to run to Hopwell, but at the sight of doña Jacinta following him, gloomy and downtrodden as a prisoner, she stood there mute with surprise. A thousand strange ideas coursed through her mind.

"What happened?" she murmured. "Here is the Espagnolette coming back alone. Her eyes are red with tears and the Cachupin is nowhere to be seen! My master is somber. He looks like he did in his bad days."

In fact, Hopwell seemed quite agitated. He led doña Jacinta to the old house where she had lived with her husband before the journey and returned to his own house almost immediately. His face betrayed as much worry as fatigue; he ate something rapidly and withdrew to his bedroom. Cora watched him with an attentive eye, trying to understand what was happening but not daring to ask him a single question. She heard him striding about and rifling through papers in his room, whose door he had closed to her. Realizing that there was nothing to be gleaned from him, Cora went prowling around the little house. Doña Jacinta remained kneeling by the window, her forehead resting on her hands, praying with fervor. Night approached; a reddish light illuminated the trees with its reflection; light, transparent clouds, colored by the last rays of the sun, stretched in regular lines across the azure sky; some tardy hummingbirds still buzzed in the cups of the flowers, and the fireflies began to glow beneath the leaves like errant stars. Hidden in a thicket, Cora watched with a malevolent curiosity the Cachupin's wife as her prayers intermingled with muffled moans. She took pleasure in hearing the sobs of the desperate woman, whose mysterious return had caused her even more anger than her arrival had inspired alarm. Like a snake whose venom becomes more potent as the temperature rises, Cora's hatred for the Cachupin's wife redoubled in the warm atmosphere of this spring evening. She was about to leave her hiding place and confront doña Jacinta head-on when she heard the sound of footsteps; she saw her master walk up and knock on the door of the house where doña Jacinta was kneeling.

Doña Jacinta arose from her knees, trembling all over. "What is it, Mr. Hopwell?" she asked in a shaky voice.

"Señora," he replied, "there is no news. We won't hear anything new for two or three days. Please be brave."

"I feel braver than I would have imagined, for indeed I have not died of sorrow," the Cachupin's wife said, "but as time passes, I lose hope."

"Yet perhaps the moment is near where you will forget your anguish. Soon the one you love and who loves you will be returned to your affections, and you will spend many peaceful days together right here. Today's torments will make tomorrow's happiness even sweeter."

"Then you still have hope?" doña Jacinta asked with a sort of exaltation.

"Yes, I do have hope," Hopwell replied.

"Ah!" doña Jacinta cried. "You are calm, you are self-possessed, Mr. Hopwell. But me, I lose my head. What will become of me, alone in the world, without support, without affection?"

"No matter what happens, rest assured, señora, I will not abandon you. This plantation already belongs to you—you are at home here. I have decided to leave these parts, but not until you have found your husband. If don Pepo does not reappear, I myself will take you back to your family."

Hopwell withdrew, and doña Jacinta, a bit calmer, went to sit in an armchair near the window. Her eyes kept turning involuntarily toward the paths from the forest, even though the darkness of night prevented her from distinguishing anything at this distance. Then Cora emerged from her hiding place and approached her.

"You do not seem well, madame," she said in a caressing voice. "Is there anything I can do for you?"

"Ah! There is nothing you can do for me," the Cachupin's wife said. "You cannot return to me what I have lost!"

"What have you lost then, dear madame?"

"My husband, don Pepo!"

"Really!" Cora said, sitting on the ground at doña Jacinta's knees. "Don Pepo is lost! How terrible!"

"He fell into the water at night."

"Oh, poor madame! He fell just like that, all alone . . . and nobody saw him?"

"No one. Mr. Hopwell had just left him—"

"Ahh! they were together then on the deck of the boat? This is what happens to a man with a beautiful wife!"

As she spoke, Cora wrapped her hands around her knees and rocked back and forth. Then she added, "I knew it would end up this way!"

"I don't understand you," doña Jacinta said.

"You don't know my master, madame. You don't know what this terrible man whom you call Mr. Hopwell has done, and what he is capable of doing. First of all, that is not his real name—"

"What does his name matter? We know what he has done. He has welcomed us and treated us like family."

"Yes, yes . . . and I repeat, it had to end up this way. I was expecting it! Don't you see, don Pepo fell into the Red River because someone helped him to. Do you think that someone your husband's age would let himself slide into the water like a child?"

"My God!" doña Jacinta cried. "If you are telling the truth—"

"And why wouldn't I be telling the truth? Because I am not white? But there is white blood in these veins, madame! When they sold me, when I was fifteen, at the market in New Orleans, I was worth more than most of the other girls in the city and my master had to pay dearly for me!"

"Please leave me alone," doña Jacinta replied. "What you are saying is none of my business."

"But what has just happened is my business. My master wanted to get rid of the Cachupin so he could have his wife. If you marry him, I am no longer anything here. I will have to be your humble servant, and that is something I do not want to be—"

"Go away, I say," doña Jacinta declared imperiously. "You have insulted me and accused your master of an odious crime!"

"Little madame," Cora said as she rose, "please listen to me! If my master has good manners, it is because he comes from a noble family, but it is no less true that he has also been a slave trader, a pirate, and who knows what else. He has done much evil in his life. None of this matters to me. I was as proud to belong to him as if he had been the most honest man in the world. I was never taught about virtue when I was a child, and my master never remedied my education."

"You are an evil creature," doña Jacinta said indignantly.

"That may well be, madame, but it is not my fault. Since he rescued you in the forest, my master has taken on great airs, he has treated me with disdain, and all of his kindness has been for you and your husband. Why would he have acted like that unless it was to trick you both? He was bored with me and you pleased him! It hurts me to admit it, but after all, you are beautiful, and your husband was in the way."

Doña Jacinta said nothing; Cora's insidious revelations had given birth in her mind to suspicions that she sought vainly to dispel. This man whom she believed to have seen a generous protector, a devoted friend—was he really a monster, her husband's assassin? There was a native distinction in Hopwell's manners; clearly he belonged to a noble race, but hadn't himself spoken of his youthful blunders? Hadn't he said "I have a past to atone for"? These reflections plunged the Cachupin's wife into new anguish. Once again she despaired of her husband's return and trembled at the thought of finding herself at the mercy of a treacherous stranger capable of any crime.

"Cora," she said finally, "if you are lying, then you are truly evil. Your words have redoubled my worries, and I no longer feel safe here—"

"Madame," Cora replied, "you found me too frank earlier when I told you about myself. Why would I be less so when talking about my master? Maybe he means to live like a Quaker for the present, but ultimately here you are alone with him, and abandoned as you are, you will have to marry him."

"Never! Never!" the Cachupin's wife said.

"You say that now, but we will soon see. Do you really think that it is easy to resist my master when he has set his mind on something? His plan was irrevocably decreed the minute he threw don Pepo into the abyss."

"I am lost, then," doña Jacinta said, "left without any defenses against a man capable of anything!"

"Madame," Cora said, "let me help. If he has his plans, I have mine as well."

Then Cora disappeared, leaving doña Jacinta even more tormented and hopeless than ever. The Cachupin's wife spent the night suffering the cruelest fear alone in the isolated house, which she locked up tight as if she were frightened of being attacked. The next day, when Hopwell invited her to have breakfast with him, she refused, alleging that she was too ill. Towards noon, Hopwell went to pay her a visit; she remained mute and confused in his presence. In vain he tried to reassure her; she trembled as if she were in the presence of an enemy and then suddenly burst out sobbing.

"Sir," she said, "let me leave this place! Have my mule saddled and I will go by myself through the forest to return to Mexico and my natural protectors."

"Not yet, señora," Hopwell said politely. "Tonight or tomorrow at the latest we will have news of don Pepo, and then it will be time to take action."

Then Hopwell withdrew, surprised at this sharp language whose significance he did not immediately grasp. After a moment's reflection he guessed that some suspicion might have developed in doña Jacinta's troubled thoughts. Although deeply hurt to find himself the target of such a terrible accusation, he preferred to remain silent rather than undertake a useless justification. All afternoon he rode through the forest paths, hoping to see some of the people he had sent out in search of don Pepo. Towards evening he returned, quite worried at not having received any news of the Cachupin. Hopwell decided to set off in search of him the next morning. At dinnertime he entered the dining room and sat down at the table that Cora had just served. She eagerly offered him a glass of ale as black as ink, topped off with a thick yellow foam. He swallowed it in a single gulp and quickly ate several slices of smoked beef. Cora, standing in a corner of the room, kept her eyes fixed upon him; she moved stealthily step by step toward the door, and when Hopwell, struck by a ghastly pallor, rose abruptly, crying, "Cora, what did you put in my glass?" she fled to the edge of the forest.

VI

There are in the movements of every creature who has just committed a criminal action manifest signs of fear and turmoil. At first Cora ran straight to the forest; then, frightened by the growing darkness, she came back to huddle near the edge of the woods beneath a thick bush. She placed her hand on her heart to try to slow its pounding beat; burning tears ran down her cheeks, and the curious gaze of the little birds who watched her attentively through the leaves was more than she could bear. Soon the sound of horse's hooves rang out behind her. Cora, trembling all over, almost fainted when she recognized the Cachupin arriving at a full gallop. He was riding a small borrowed horse that was so weary that its four legs seemed to be moving only at the rider's instigation. As soon as he emerged into the clearing, don Pepo began to shout with all his might: "Jacinta! Jacinta!" At the sound of this cry, repeated by all the echoes of the forest, doña Jacinta dashed out of the house. Shaking with emotion, she took a few steps forward, but a nervous trembling seized her entire body and she felt on the verge of swooning. A vague fear countered her joy; she was experiencing that terrible anxiety of a troubled soul that can no longer distinguish dream from reality.

"Jacinta!" the Cachupin repeated as he leapt off his horse. "Wake up! It's me, it's Pepo!"

Doña Jacinta let out a cry of joy and tearfully threw herself into her husband's arms.

Cora, frozen by surprise and fear at the foot of the bush that hid her from sight, had seen the desolate woman, whose soul she had taken such pleasure in filling with terror and cruel worry, return to life and happiness. That was the first punishment for her crime. Since doña Jacinta's husband had reappeared, what good was it to have poisoned her master? If Hopwell were tired of the life he led in this wilderness, without other company than that of a woman of color, it became clear that his conduct toward the Cachupin and doña Jacinta hid no disloyal intentions. These reflections crossed Cora's narrow mind, but remorse found no place in her soul, overwhelmed as it was by tumultuous passions. Like a poorly tamed lioness who, in a moment of capricious fury, mortally wounds the keeper whose hands and feet she had licked every day and then runs roaring from her cage, Cora, drunk with anger, began to flee through the forest without knowing where she was going.

Night had fallen; the Cachupin, surprised not to see any light coming from Hopwell's house and not to have seen him appear upon his arrival, hurried to knock at his door. A weak voice responded: "Come in!" The Cachupin entered the dining room, and in the middle of a profound darkness his hand met the frozen hand of his host.

"What has happened? What is wrong with you?" the Cachupin replied.

"Call doña Jacinta," Hopwell replied. "I must speak to both of you."

Don Pepo returned as quickly as possible, accompanied by doña Jacinta. They had brought a light that, illuminating Hopwell's ghastly features, revealed the tragic truth.

"I am dying!" he said. "Where is Cora? She has disappeared, hasn't she? Don't pursue her. I forgive her for her crime. Although I was unable to elevate this savage creature to my own level, I do not have to lower myself to hers—"

"But we must call a doctor immediately!" the Cachupin said. "We will find this hateful woman later."

"The doctor is far away," Hopwell said, "and death approaches quickly. The poison she gave me comes from the coast of Africa. Its effects are rapid and without remedy. Give me your hand, my friend. . . . Excuse me, señora, if I make you witness this sad scene, when you have not even had time to recover from your last anxieties. . . . This plantation legally belongs to you. At the bottom of the deed I indicated that you had paid me in advance. You thus own this free and clear. Before you arrived, I was shamefully vegetating in an evil and unregulated life. I don't even know if my intentions were good in bringing you here. But seeing you in the midst of this misery, happy in the affection that unites you, I reexamined myself and understood that I was on the wrong path. My name is not the one I told you, but what does it matter? It must remain unknown, for my family has cursed me. Having lost vast sums of money gambling, I set off on adventures. I was a slave trader and a privateer. Señora, please forgive a dying man who seeks to redeem his sins. I did not kill your husband as you perhaps thought. I excuse the suspicions that may have sprung up in your troubled mind, but it was I who attacked and captured the *Mariposa*. Your father perished in the struggle. It is a misfortune that I cannot possibly make amends for. But at least accept as indemnity for the loss of the ship all that you will find in my coffers. 'He who lives by the sword dies by the sword,' say the Gospels. He who has for so long risked the lives of his fellow men must die a violent death."

Doña Jacinta, terror-stricken to find herself face to face with the man who had killed her father, withdrew from Hopwell in horror.

"Señora," the dying man said, making an effort to turn toward her, "will you join your curses with those my family has heaped upon me, and which will be fulfilled today? The sufferings of a soul with nothing to regret cannot compare to those of a heart tormented by remorse! But repentance is like fire—it can purify all."

As Hopwell spoke, his contorted features regained their habitual calm. The cruel suffering against which he had been fighting for an hour lessened by degrees; one would have said that he was giving in to sleep. Little by little his eyes closed; he fell into a deep oblivion; his black hair set into relief the whiteness of his brow, furrowed by premature wrinkles. His head thrown back on his chair, legs crossed, arms hanging down, he seemed to be dreaming and reliving scenes of his childhood, where the spirit finds refuge in solemn moments, for they bring back the days of candor and innocence. The doctor the Cachupin had sent for could not arrive until the next day toward noon. It was too late; Cora's poison had accomplished its ends with a frightening rapidity. The doctor took Hopwell's hand and declared that he had been dead since morning.

If the dead man had pardoned his executioner, justice could not renounce her own prosecution. They began to search actively for Cora in all directions. The old, white-haired black man who waited with his companion at the edge of the Sabine to take passengers across in his ferry declared that a young woman of color, almost white, had asked for passage across the river, but he had refused to take her to the Mexican shore. It became more or less certain that Cora was wandering in the marshes that bordered the Sabine. After having searched the lowlands covered in somber cypress for four or five days, the sheriff discovered a flock of vultures circling lower and lower toward the ground. This was the sign of a dead body, and sheriff headed in that direction. He was struck by a hideous spectacle. A cadaver was stretched out on the muddy earth; it was Cora, who had starved to death in the wilderness. Her shredded clothes barely covered the body formerly full of life and youth, now sullied with filth and the victim of birds of prey. Her white muslin handkerchief, snatched by the hooked claw of a vulture, was covered in blood, and a preliminary peck of the beak had already attacked the black eye that had shot forth flashes of passion and jealous fury only days before.

NOTES

INTRODUCTION

1. The annotated text of the Jefferson-Madison correspondence regarding the Louisiana-Texas border dispute is found in James Morton Smith, ed., *The Republic of Letters: The Correspondence between Thomas Jefferson and James Madison 1776–1826*, vol. 3 (New York: W. W. Norton, 1995). For the complete text of the letters exchanged between Gen. James Wilkinson and Gen. Simón de Herrera and Gov. Antonio Cordero, see "The Neutral Ground Agreement: October 29 and November 4, 1806" in Ernest Wallace, David M. Vigness, George B. Ward, eds., *Documents of Texas History*, 2d ed. (Austin: State House Press, 1994), pp. 37–38.

2. Herbert Eugene Bolton, the University of Texas historian who articulated the concept of the floating Spanish Borderlands and collected and translated many of the basic documents, supervised the writing of the definitive treatment of the Adams-Onís Treaty. See Bolton's student Brooks for the history and text of the treaty. Philip Coolidge Brooks, *Diplomacy in the Borderlands: The Adams-Onís Treaty of 1819*, vol 24 (Berkeley: University of California Press, 1939).

3. See Walter F. McCaleb, *The Aaron Burr Conspiracy;* and *A New Light on Aaron Burr*, expanded ed., with an introduction by Charles A. Beard and a new introduction by the author (New York: Argosy-Antiquarian, 1966).

4. In this book, "Creole" is used in the meaning current in 1829–30, when Théodore Pavie made the trip that provided him with the settings for these stories. A Creole is a person of pure Spanish or French descent, born in America. "Borderlands" refers to the Sabine Borderlands, a fixed geographic region which, for a long period (including the time during which Pavie's stories are set), coincided with the floating Spanish borderlands of Herbert Eugene Bolton.

5. John Durst (1797–1851), East Texas merchant and patriot who owned the structure built by the founder of modern Nacogdoches, Antonio Gil y Barbo, lived there with his family at the time of Pavie's visit. Durst spoke English, Spanish, French, German, and several Indian languages, including Cherokee. He negotiated the terms that spared the life of Colonel Piedras after the 1832 Battle of Nacogdoches. When Durst learned of the approach of Santa Anna, he rode 960 miles on horseback warning the people of Texas, earning the sobriquet "the Paul Revere of Texas." Joe E. and Carolyn Reeves Ericson, "John Durst," in Ron C. Tyler et al., eds., *The New Handbook of Texas* (Austin: Texas State Historical Association, 1996), 2:736–37.

6. For a translation of the southern portion of *Souvenirs atlantiques* and a biography of Théodore Pavie see Betje Black Klier, *Pavie in the Borderlands* (Baton Rouge: Louisiana State University Press, forthcoming).

7. It is preceded in time by a novel set at Champ d'Asile, the Texas Bonapartist colony generally believed to have been near present-day Liberty or Moss Bluff. *L'Héroïne du Texas* was published in Paris anonymously in 1819. Though the author claimed to have been an eyewitness, some scholars (myself included) believe that it was written in Paris by a literary hack who gleaned information from newspapers and other publications, who may or may not have had conversations with returning colonists. Several publicity pieces aimed at drawing immigrants or colonists to Texas, as well as publications with political or religious agendas, predate "Le Lazo." They were not written to entertain the reader. The most conspicuous example is Timothy Flint's *Francis Berrian; or the Mexican Patriot*, a two-volume novel published in Boston in 1826, which Sister Agatha [M. Agatha Sheehan] in her *Study of the First Four Novels of Texas* (Washington, 1939) calls "nothing but a loosely connected diatribe against the Spanish-Catholic culture" (cited in Thomas W. Streeter, *United States and European Imprints relating to Texas*, pt. 3, vol. 2 of *Bibliography of Texas, 1795–1845* (Cambridge: Harvard University Press, 1955–60), p. 75.

8. See Don Graham et al., eds., *The Texas Literary Tradition: Fiction, Folklore, History* (Austin: University of Texas Press, 1983).

9. The myth of Prometheus, who rebelled against a tyrannical Zeus and brought fire (a symbol of knowledge) to mankind, was dear to the French Romantics who felt the need to revolt against many kinds of literary controls, including censorship. The German sculptor, Elisabet Ney, portrayed Pavie's friend Victor Hugo as Prometheus. Though slightly damaged, this work is on display at Ney's studio in Austin, Texas.

10. Pavie seems to have written several passages in *Souvenirs atlantiques* for the purpose of redeeming the tarnished reputation which Chateaubriand was suffering at that time. His young admirer confirmed or illustrated portions of *Atala, René*, and *The Natchez*, books which he carried with him on his journey. "Le Nègre" may have been written to illustrate a passage from *The Natchez* in which one of the characters is "received by the Blacks, his companions in servitude, with singing and dancing: the night was spent in this merriment of chains." François René, vicomte de Chateaubriand, *The Natchez*, vol. 2 (London: Henry Colburn, 1827; reprint, New York: Howard Fertig, 1978) p. 196.

11. The history of the Vendée region during the counterrevolution waged by Catholic royalists against the Republican army is filled with stories of people hiding in forests, grottoes, and hollow logs. One vividly illustrated collection of these stories is *Blancs et Bleus dans la Vendée déchirée* (Paris: Découvertes Gallimard, 1993), p. 107. In addition to reading such stories in the works of Balzac and Hugo, Théodore would certainly have heard similar tales in the Pavie household. His grandmother was imprisoned during the Terror, and both

of the faithful servants who stayed with the family through several generations are known to have filled his childhood with revolutionary stories.

12. Charles Augustin Sainte-Beuve (1804–69) was an intimate friend of the Pavie brothers and France's most significant literary critic during the nineteenth century. Prior to World War I, when the function of literary criticism changed profoundly, his doctrine was influential in the United States and Britain also. For many years, Théodore paid weekly visits to Sainte-Beuve, who introduced him to Orientalist Eugène Bournouf and to François Buloz (1804–77), the editor-in-chief of the *Revue des Deux Mondes.*

13. François-René, vicomte de Chateaubriand (1768–1848), the aristocratic uncle of Alexis de Tocqueville, escaped to America for a short time during the French Revolution. His most popular novels, *René* and *Atala,* inspired Pavie and numerous other travelers to visit Louisiana. During his diplomatic career, Chateaubriand meddled in Texas and Mexican politics in an unsuccessful attempt to restore Bourbon rule in the Spanish colonies.

14. Honoré de Balzac (1799–1850), one of France's most prolific novelists and author of *La Comédie humaine,* was intensely interested in Texas because he was living in Paris during the time of the fund-raising campaign for the Bonapartist colony on the Trinity River at Champ d'Asile, Texas. Instead of taking a personal journey, the unrivaled master-of-plots later dispatched one of his characters to Champ d'Asile in his novel, *La Rabouilleuse.* Historians often appreciate Balzac's astute social observations, disregarding—or treasuring—the fictional elements that represent a different realm of "truth."

15. Spaniards remaining in Mexico after its independence from Spain were called "gachupín" or "gachupines." Because Pavie uses "El," the Spanish equivalent of "the" in his story's title, instead of the French "Le" (and because he spoke perfect Spanish), we may presume that he is providing a French transliteration or phonetic equivalent, "cachupin," to permit the francophone reader to imagine correctly the sound of the Spanish word. "Gachupín" had taken on scurrilous connotations by 1829–30. Anglos in Texas and Louisiana called the same group "the dons," with similar disdain.

16. In the interval between the publication of these two fictional stories in the *Revue des Deux Mondes,* the tragic fate of two Texas colonies, founded separately by prominent French journalist-politicians Étienne Cabet and Victor Considerant, kept Texas in the forefront of French consciousness for the decade. By then, Pavie was a highly respected travel writer and scholar, and a professor of Sanskrit at the Collège de France.

17. Théodore Pavie, *Scènes et Récits des Pays d'Outremer* (Paris: Michel Lévy Frères, 1853), pp. 186–226. "La Peau d'ours" was also published in Münster, Germany in 1856 in *Nouvelles pittoresques: Bibliothèque gediegener und interessanter französischer Werke,* vol. 8.

18. Two of Pavie's tales from this collection served both as inspiration and source materials for the opera, *Lakmé.* Charles P. D. Cronin and Betje Black Klier,

"Théodore Pavie's *'Les Babouches du bramane,'* and the Story of Delibes's *Lakmé*," *Opera Quarterly* 12, no. 4 (Summer, 1996): 19–33.

19. "El Cachupin" is one of four stories in a collection of stories for Americans studying French. *Contes de la Vie Rustique* (New York: William R. Jenkins, 1899), 199–221.

I. LE NÈGRE

1. The French title has been retained to avoid the negative connotations in the English cognate. Evidence that Pavie had *Bug Jargal* on his mind before he arrived in Nacogdoches is found by pairing a song mentioned in *Souvenirs atlantiques* with an incident in Victor Hugo's *Bug Jargal:* "One day as I entered he took no notice of me; he was seated with his back to the door of the cell, and was whistling in melancholy mood the Spanish air, 'Yo que soy contrabandista.' ['A smuggler am I.']" This song signaled the slave uprising in Saint-Domingue in 1804. In *Souvenirs atlantiques,* Pavie attributes this song to a wagoneer he meets on the road from Natchitoches to Nacogdoches. It is doubtful that Pavie actually heard Mexicans singing this song; it is far more likely that he included it as a tribute to Victor Hugo. See "Sabine" in Betje Klier's *Pavie in the Borderlands* (Baton Rouge: Louisiana State University Press, forthcoming).

2. In this description of the marshes, Pavie differentiates between "moustiques," the standard French word for mosquitoes, and "maringouins." In his study of Louisiana French, linguist William A. Read identifies the former as a small house mosquito and the latter as a large swamp mosquito. Pavie joins a long line of French travel writers since 1655, including Cavelier de La Salle and Pénicaut, to mention this pest. William A. Read, *Louisiana French* (Baton Rouge: Louisiana State University Press, 1931), pp. 92–95.

3. "Griffe" is a term without apparent English equivalent for a person of blended race. According to Gary Mills, the percentage is three-quarters Negro, one-quarter white. Gary B. Mills, *The Forgotten People: Cane River's Creoles of Color* (Baton Rouge: Louisiana State University Press), p. xiii.

2. LE LAZO

1. Carlos E. Castañeda, *Our Catholic Heritage in Texas,* vol. 6 (Austin, Tex.: Von Boeckmann-Jones, 1950), pp. 331–34.

2. Texas historians generally focus on the complaints against Piedras documented in the Nacogdoches archives. They range from false arrest, brutality, misappropriation of funds, and cattle theft to monopolizing trade with the troops and causing hardship for the local merchants. James Gallaway Partin, "A History of Nacogdoches and Nacogdoches County, Texas, to 1877" (master's thesis, University of Texas at Austin, 1968). To these, Margaret Swett Henson adds arrogant acts like arresting an old man because he did not move quickly and ordering the repositioning of houses to meet traditional Spanish regulations

about street grids (personal communication, October, 1997). In September, 1829, Piedras reported to his superior that his men were short of ammunition and had not been paid for eleven months (Partin, p. 160). His position was entirely exposed, since he had no fortifications and the presidio depended on subsistence stores obtained through American merchants in Natchitoches. "I do not anticipate an invasion on the part of the Government of the U.S. of the North, but an outbreak countenanced by that Government of the Colonists. . . . [T]he sacrifice of my own and my fellow soldiers' lives could not prevent the triumph of those who have been plotting long beforehand the occupation of this portion of the Republic, and are now satisfied that their projects may be easily realized by cutting me off from means of subsistence, and from the assistance the troops stationed in the interior of the country" (Partin, pp. 160–61).

3. George Lewis Crocket, *Two Centuries in East Texas: A History of San Augustine County and Surrounding Territory from 1685 to the Present Time* (Dallas, Tex.: Southwest Press, 1932), p. 66. The name of Matheo Antonio Gil y Barbo, the founder of modern Nacogdoches, has numerous spellings, including Ybarbo, Ybarvo, Ibarbo, and Ibarvo, which is most common today. Following Chabot, who alphabetizes "Gil Ybarbo" under "G," I prefer a spelling that reflects the family genealogy. Frederick C. Chabot, *With the Makers of San Antonio* (San Antonio, Tex.: Artes Gráficas, 1937), pp. 216–18.

4. Théodore Pavie, Natchitoches, Louisiana, to Louis Pavie, Angers, France, Feb. 23, 1830. Klier, *Pavie in the Borderlands.*

5. This revolution, which took place on the "three glorious days" of July 27, 28, and 29, ousted the Bourbon family definitively from the French throne, just as the Battle of Nacogdoches two years later ousted the Mexican military from East Texas. These revolutions were not as complete as they might seem; the new king, Louis-Philippe, was a Bourbon on his mother's side, and a sizable portion of the population of East Texas today is Mexican American.

6. Hugh Honour, *Romanticism* (N.Y.: Harper and Row, 1979), pp. 242–43.

7. Betje Klier's translations of selected chapters of the first edition of *Souvenirs atlantiques.* "Atlantic Memories," *Southern Humanities Review* 26, no. 3 (Summer, 1992): 215–28.

8. Ibid., p. 225.

9. A lithograph made from George Stubb's well-known painting is still in the possession of Pavie's heirs.

10. Louisiana biologist William D. Reese speculated that the sweet-gum roots might have been thrown into the fire, so that the fragrant burning resin would repel mosquitoes. Sweet gum was well known for the resin it produces, which in those days was an item of commerce known as "copal." Copal was used for its sweet aroma as incense when it burned. Personal communication, Feb. 17, 1998.

11. A "pavillon chinois"—also called a Turkish crescent or jingling Johnny—is a military percussion instrument consisting of a staff with bells that jingle when the staff is struck against the ground.

3. LA PEAU D'OURS

1. For details on the precipitating episodes of these events from December through March, see Archie P. MacDonald's "Fredonian Rebellion" in Ron C. Tyler et al., eds., *The New Handbook of Texas* (Austin: Texas State Historical Association, 1996), 2:1163–64. Ernest William Winkler addresses the large question of land claims in "The Cherokee Indians in Texas," *The Quarterly of the Texas State Historical Association* 7, no. 2 (October, 1903): 95–165. See also Dianna Everett, *The Texas Cherokees: A People between Two Fires, 1819–1840* (Norman: University of Oklahoma Press, 1990). Everett tells the story within an elaborate cultural framework.

2. Numerous bands of Cherokees, displaced from their homeland "in the wild and picturesque region where the present states of Tennessee, Alabama, Georgia, and the Carolinas join one another" by the American Revolution and Anglo American settlers, moved into Louisiana, "the territory of their friend and ally Spain" (Winkler, "Cherokee Indians," p. 95). Temporarily in Arkansas after the United States purchased Louisiana, the Cherokees sought refuge in Texas under the Spanish aegis in 1819, about the time the United States renounced to Spain its claims on Texas by negotiating and signing the Adams-Onís Treaty with Spain. Spain did not ratify the treaty, however, until 1821, when Mexico achieved its independence.

3. Fields's father-in-law was François "Touline" Grappe, a well-known Natchitoches trader and frequent interpreter and negotiator among these competing entities. Though Grappe died in August, 1825, he left some eighty children and grandchildren, many in Campti near the plantation of Charles Pavie. The proximity of these relations might explain the rapidity with which the news of the cessation of Indian hostilities crossed the Sabine in Pavie's fiction. Elizabeth Mills, to whom I am grateful for information on Natchitoches history, provides the genealogy and a brief biography of Grappe in her study of Athanase de Mézières. Elizabeth Shown Mills, "De Mézières-Trichel-Grappe: A Study of a Tri-Caste Lineage in the Old South," *The Genealogist* 6, no. 1 (Spring, 1985): 4–84.

4. Winkler ("Cherokee Indians," pp. 98, 108) presents a translation from the Bexar Archives of the 1823 document from Minister Lucas Alamán that both confirms and undermines the agreement with Colonel Trespalacios. Alamán communicated to the provisional governor of Texas that their "Supreme Highnesses" advised that the agreement was to "remain provisionally in force [but that he was required nevertheless to be] careful and, in regard to their [Cherokee tribal] settlements, endeavoring to bring them towards the interior, at places least dangerous." His instructions reserve the possibility of reneging on the agreement which encouraged the Cherokees to improve the land and keep Americans out, and they reflect the capital's ignorance of or disregard for the Cherokee culture, the nature of Texas geography, and the human investment

involved in establishing an agrarian settlement from which the hunters made sorties.

5. Ibid., p. 112.
6. Ibid., p. 111. In all of his separationist activities, Fields was supported by Dr. John Dunn Hunter, a white man raised by Indians. Hunter sought to establish a separate Indian nation in Texas in defiance of Mexican authorities. Fields and Hunter exercised the same loyalties, signed the same treaties, and shared the same unfortunate fate.
7. Nacogdoches Archives, in Everett, *Texas Cherokees*, p. 43.
8. B. W. Edwards to Aylett C. Buckner, December 26, 1826, in Winkler, "Cherokee Indians," pp. 143–44.
9. Ibid., p. 147.
10. Ibid., p. 148.
11. Everett points out the unfortunate future consequences of Bowles's loyalty to Piedras: "The Cherokee's apparent willingness to help the Mexican against Texan would incense the Americans living around Nacogdoches." The Cherokees never gained title to their East Texas lands in spite of the efforts of their adopted son, Sam Houston. In summer, 1839, when Mirabeau B. Lamar was president of the Republic of Texas, a Texas ranger shot Bowles in the head at point-blank range during a skirmish preceding the removal of the Texas Cherokees to present-day Oklahoma. Everett, *Texas Cherokees*, pp. 64–65.
12. Théodore Pavie, *Souvenirs atlantiques* (Angers: Pavie Press, 1832), p. 145.
13. E. E. Rich, *The History of the Hudson's Bay Company, 1670–1870* (London: The Hudson's Bay Record Society, 1959), p. 398.
14. *La Grande Encyclopédie Larousse*, 1972 ed., s.v. "Canada," "Simpson."
15. I have a copy of an unpublished manuscript titled "The Plantation" with more detailed descriptions of Charles and Marianne Pavie and their adopted daughter Marie Eliza Bludworth, who was always called Élise. The planters and plantation complexes in the unpublished story and this one strongly resemble each other.
16. Marie Eliza Bludworth married Edward Orlando Blanchard on May 18, 1835. She inherited her adopted father Charles Pavie's *Ile aux vâches* plantation when he died in 1838. This plantation included both sides of the Cane River, extending nearly to Grand Écore. After having two children (Charles Pavie Blanchard and Marie Eliza Blanchard) whose descendants live in the Natchitoches area and throughout Louisiana today, Eliza, Théodore Pavie's first love, died at the age of thirty-three after giving birth to twins who apparently did not survive. Marie Norris Wise, *Norris-Jones-Crockett, Payne, Blanchard: The Heritage of Marie Norris Wise* (Sulphur, La.: Wise Publications, 1994), pp. 71–74.
17. In the 1820s, Natchitoches was still the principal river port for merchandise moving overland to Nacogdoches or San Antonio. Spanish law prevented commercial transfer by Texas ports on the Gulf of Mexico, the logical overland route to San Antonio. Political and geographic changes in the next two decades

would destroy that pattern. Changes in the political situation in Texas joined alterations in the course of the Red River in the 1830s, caused by the removal of the "raft" (logjam) above Natchitoches by U.S. engineer Henry Miller Shreve (1785–1851). The dominant commercial role of Natchitoches shifted to Shreveport and Galveston.

18. Pavie added parenthetically, "rivers are roads that move, said Pascal."

19. "Père," meaning "father," was a polite yet familiar way for men to address an older man who did not have the social standing to be addressed as "monsieur" plus family name, but whose age commanded some mark of respect beyond calling him by his last name. The quaint custom of using "monsieur" or "mister" with the given name, just as the young Creole woman calls père Faustin's son "Mr. Antoine," continued into the twentieth century in Natchitoches. I heard the young cousins of one of the descendants of these Canadian settlers address an octogenarian as "Mr. Alphonse." He was distantly related by marriage to the historical planter on whom the character is modeled.

20. According to Carl A. Brasseaux, Center for Louisiana Studies, University of Southwestern Louisiana, Upper Louisiana is usually defined as that portion of colonial above the 31st parallel. That would include the Arkansas post, present-day Missouri, the Illinois country, and the settlements along the Ohio River. Lower Louisiana included all of the settlements below the 31st parallel: Natchitoches, Pointe Coupée, the German Coast, New Orleans, and the English Turn area settlements. During the 1760s—the late French period—Opelousas, Attakapas, the lower Acadian Coast, and Rapides were added. Ouachita, Lafourche, Avoyelles, and the second Acadian Coast were added during the Spanish period. During the French colonial period, the settlements of Biloxi, Pascagoula, and Mobile also fell into this category. They were considered part of West Florida after British occupation of Trans-Appalachian Louisiana in 1764. (Personal correspondence, May, 1997.)

21. Habitants and habitations in the Creole language are synonymous for planters and plantations. (Notation in original collection by Pavie; hereafter Pavie's notations will be designated with [TP].) Exchanging handshakes, an American style of greeting, would be a touch of American local color to a French reader.

22. The bald cypress *(Schubertia disticha)* grows plentifully along the banks of the Mississippi and its tributaries. It is covered with a black moss, several feet long, which Americans call "long moss" and Creoles call "Spanish beard" [TP].

23. Name given to the Creoles who cultivate a small expanse of land themselves [TP]. They are also known as yeoman farmers or self-employed farmers. In the South they called themselves self-working farmers, because they had only their family members to help with farm tasks. Squatters settled on the land they worked to stake their claim and await title.

24. Read *(Louisiana French,* p. 133) says that most Creoles and Acadians use the word "caiman" for the large alligator with prominent scales, reserving "cocodrie" for a smaller type, quite slender and covered with nearly smooth scales.

Although some speakers of French use "crocodile" for every kind of alligator, Pavie (who saw alligators in the Nile after he visited Louisiana) distinguishes between caiman and alligator. Like the passenger pigeons, the parrots (Carolina Parroquets) are extinct today. Pavie rhapsodises on them in *Souvenirs atlantiques.*

25. Pavie well understood the magnitude of the Sabine River, but English does not usually make the distinction between the French "rivière" and "fleuve." Both are usually translated as "river," though a fleuve may be called a "great river." A rivière flows into a fleuve that carries it to an ocean or sea. The Seine, the Loire, the Amazon, and the Nile—all waters on which Pavie had sailed by the time he wrote this story—are fleuves, as are the Mississippi and the Sabine. It is within this group that the Sabine is considered small, as he called it in French.

26. House built of barely hewn tree trunks [TP].

27. Bustards: name that Creoles give to the hyperborean goose [TP], Canada or snow geese.

28. Wheat and cornflowers symbolize Canada at its best. Bluebonnets and Indian paintbrush would be equivalent in Texas culture and folklore.

29. At the base of the wing of the Louisiana starling (the American rice bird) is an epaulet of a beautiful red color [TP]. (This apparently is the red-winged blackbird.)

30. Reference to a prodigious wedding feast celebrating a peasant's marriage in *Don Quixote.*

31. The French expression "donner un coup de main" means both "to lend a hand," as the Indians of the Mississippi Valley often did for French settlers, and "to strike" or "slap" them, which they likewise did occasionally. The phrase's ambiguity captures the uncertainty of the situation.

32. An equestrian demonstration of Arab horsemen who execute on the gallop various evolutions while discharging their firearms and emitting loud cries. In 1833, Eugène Delacroix, a friend of the Pavie brothers, titled one of his paintings "Fantasia" from the Arabic "fantaziya," meaning ostentation. Paul Robert, *Le Petit Robert Dictionnaire,* A. Rey and J. Rey-Debove, eds., (Paris: Société du Nouveau Littré, 1979).

33. Pavie names two trees that might easily be mistaken for their cognates: lilas de Chine and jasmine. He identifies lilas de Chine elsewhere as *Melia azadarch,* which we know as the chinaberry tree. Berlandier had noted chinaberry trees at San Felipe de Austin in 1827, saying that locals "improperly called [them] Louisiana lilacs." Jean-Louis Berlandier, *Journey to Mexico during the Years 1826–1834,* vol. 2 (Austin: Texas State Historical Association, 1980), p. 321. Read (*Louisiana French,* p. 79) lists jasmine as *Asimins triloba dunal,* or pawpaw tree, which is significant because it is generally assumed today that Natchitoches originally meant "pawpaw eater." William D. Reese notes that Acadians call the pawpaw jasminier or agminier, both relating to the Indian name for the tree and also the source for the name of the genus *Asimina.* "Jessamine" is a

corruption of the plant's original Indian name—unrelated to the true "jasmines" of the botanical world. Personal correspondence, Feb. 17, 1998.

4 . EL CACHUPIN

1. For a more complete version of this story, see my article on the 1829 Spanish invasion and the 1839 Pastry War. Betje Klier, "Peste, Tempestad y Pâtisserie," *Gulf Coast Historical Review* 7, no. 2 (Spring, 1977): 59–73.

2. Although Pavie found it necessary to transfer the ferry boat to the eastern side of the Sabine River for this story, no evidence has surfaced of a Louisiana ferry, according to Carl Brasseaux and Glenn Conrad. In *Souvenirs atlantiques,* he mentions the Gaines stopover as "the shack where passersby stop."

3. When Pavie died childless in 1896, he left a substantial sum to establish a school for nuns to teach indigent women to read. Pavie's best-known tale, "Les Babouches du Brahmane," is set in India, but it explores the misfortunes of a dependent, illiterate woman cut adrift from her male support. Pavie's great respect for women and literacy no doubt stems from the success of his widowed grandmother—his surrogate mother—and the religious press she owned after the French Revolution.

4. Privateers operated under government-issued "letters of marque" during times of maritime conflict. They did not attack vessels from countries that were allies of the granting government, nor did they kill women or children. Their pay came from dividing the booty they captured, and their letters protected them from ordinary justice. When Laffite could no longer obtain letters of marque, he permitted his men to choose to continue as pirates or return to shore. For general information on Laffite, see Lyle Saxon, *LaWtte the Pirate* (New Orleans: R. L. Crager, 1950; reprint; Gretna, La.: Pelican Publishing Co., 1989).

5. The next few years were the final active years of the Baratarians. Many who continued to engage in piracy after 1821 were captured and convicted of piracy. By 1825, no privateering licenses were issued because the Latin American states that issued them had achieved their independence.

6. Pavie describes the moss as two or three "brasses," an ancient French measure of roughly five feet—approximately the length of an adult standing with both arms extended to the side, or an English "brace." Robert, *Le Petit Robert Dictionnaire.*

7. The name given in the Americas to Spaniards born in Europe [TP].

8. Because wheat flour was not available in Nacogdoches or Natchitoches, tortillas, cornbread, or cornpones were prepared from corn.

9. At this time, the village was Natchitoches and the city was New Orleans.

INDEX

Catholic, xvi, 10, 96*nn* 7, 11

Catholic church, xvi, 10. *See also* Nacogdoches

Champ d'Asile, 96*n* 7, 97*n* 14

characters, historical implications of: Antoine and Étienne, 29; Antonio, xv, 12, 15; Clara, 13; José de las Piedras, 12; Cora, 61–62; Delaware, 13, 15; Hopwell, 60–63; Jacinta, xviii, 61, 62, 63; Marie, 29; Pepo, 60–63; Père Faustin, 29–30; noble slave, xv

Chateaubriand, François René, vicomte de, xvii, 4, 62, 97*n* 13

Cherokee, 13, 26, 27, 29, 31, 100*n* 3

Coahuila, xiv, 11

Comanche, xviii–xiv, 4, 27

Conrad, Glenn, 104*n* 2

Considerant, Victor, 97*n* 16

Constitution of 1824, 11

Copal, uses of, 99*n* 10

Cordero, Gov. Antonio, 95*n* 1

Creole, xiv, 12, 15, 16, 29, 30, 60–62, 95*n* 4, 102*nn* 19, 21, 22, 23, 103*n* 27; definition 95*n* 4

Crocket, George, 12, 13, 99*n* 3

Cuba, 63

culturescape, xviii

dance: contredanse, 40; slave, 5–7

Delacroix, Eugène, 15, 103*n* 32

Durst, John, xiv, xviii, 27, 95*n* 5

East Texas, xviii, 10, 11, 26, 29, 95*n* 5, 101*n* 11

Edwards, Benjamin, 27

Edwards, Haden, 21, 26, 27

English, xiii, 60, 62, 102*n* 20

Europe, European, xiii, xv, 4, 12, 29, 97*n* 5, 102*n* 20

Everett, Dianna, 27, 100*n* 1, 101*n* 7–11

exiles: economic, xviii, 28–29; political, 60, 97*n* 16

expulsion of Spaniards, 60

"Fantasia," 103*n* 32

Far West, Le, xv

fauna: alligator (so-called "crocodiles") 5, 18, 102*n* 4; bear, 37, 46; beef, 70; bird, 35, 42, 68; birds of prey, 33, 43, 66, 94; bluejay, 64; boar, 35; buck, 41, 47; buffalo, 18, 53; buzzards, 43; caiman 38, 73, 82; cardinal, 73; cats, wild, 64; cattle, 35; cock, 85; cranes and goslings, 34; creole pony, 68; crocodile (alligators), 5, 51; deer, 75; dog, 5, 8, 35, 77; duck, 42, 43, 46; eagle, 23, 73; egret, 47; falcons, 43; fawn, spotted, 5, 68; fireflies, 87; fox squirrels, 75; game, 64; geese, 64; green parrot, 20, 22, 25; herons, 64, 81; horse, 8, 11, 14, 23, 24, 25, 35, 43, 63, 64, 68, 74, 75, 78, 80, 86, 91; hummingbird, 42, 73, 87; jackal, 58; lioness, 92; mockingbird, 59, 64, 73; mule, 64, 66, 69, 70; night bird, 52; ostriches, 24; owl, 17, 55; oxen, 53; panther, 14, 24; parrots, 38; partridge, 51; passenger pigeons, 32, 41; pigeons, 32; possum, 5; reptile, 8, 69; roe, 7; roseate spoonbill, 64; serpent, 5; snake, 87; snow geese, 44; songbirds, 73; sparrow, 42; stag, 57; starling, 47; steed, 24; swamp mosquito, 5; tortoise, 38, 82; tortoiseshell, 64; turkey, 38, 47; turtle, 5, 43, 73; venison, 70; vulture, 94; whippoorwill, 17; wildcat, 5, 18; wild duck, 84; wolves, 46; wood pigeon, 17, 43; worm, 5

Federalist, 10, 11

Ferdinand VII, 60

Fields, Chief Richard, 26–28, 100*n* 3, 101*n* 6

filibusters, xv

flora: acacia, 42; boggy lowlands, 48; brush, 66; cane, 18, 101, 104; catalpa, 17; cattails, 43, 44, 86; chinaberry, 59, 70; corn, 17, 40, 54, 70,

72, 104*n* 8; cornflowers, 45; cotton, 38, 42, 53, 55, 64; cypress, 8, 36, 43, 63, 64, 66, 69, 75, 94; foliage, 64; gourd, 4; grass, 19, 45, 35, 38, 66, 75; hanging vine, 82; liana, 42, 44; locust tree, 32, 49, 66; magnolia, 17, 43, 64, 75; maple, 36, 42; marsh, 18, 55, 60, 64, 94; moss, 66; palm, 16; palmetto, 64; palm-leaf, 36; pawpaw, 59, 82; persimmon, 18; reed, 43, 48; rushes, 58; sassafras, 38; shoals, 64; shrubs, 19; slime, 58; spiny shrub, 66; spiny vine, 83; sugarcane, 8, 9, 17, 38, 64, 81; sweet-gum, 17; sweet potato, 40; sycamore, 35, 36, 43, 73; tangled vine, 66; thick bush, 91; thicket, 43, 47, 55, 68, 75; thorny bush, 43; tobacco, 40, 54, 61, 62; tulip tree, 43; vines, 5, 75; wild cherry, 59; willow, 38, 43; yam, 17; yucca, 5

Florida, West, 102*n* 20

Fort Miró, 3

France, xiii, xiv, xv, xvi, xviii, 15, 18, 31, 62, 63

Francis Barrian (Timothy Flint), 96*n* 7

Fredonia, 27

Fredonian Rebellion, 10–11, 26, 100*n* 1

French/France, xiii–xviii passim, 29, 30, 31, 61, 62, 63; Canadian legislation against language, 29; descent, 95*n* 4; impact on Texas literature, 97*n* 13, 14, 16; intervention in Mexico, xvii; July Revolution, 15, 99*n* 5; outpost (Natchitoches), xiii; political situation in the Vendée, xvi; politics, xvi; Revolution, xvi, 96*n* 11, 104*n* 3; word for shed, 10

French Revolution, xvi

Gachupín, xvii, 11–12, 97*n* 15

Gaines Crossing and Ferry, 21, 61, 104*n* 2

Galveston, 60, 61

Georgia, 100*n* 2

Géricault, Théodore, 14

Gil y Barbo, Antonio, xiv, 12, 95*n* 5, 99*n* 3. *See also* Ybarbo, Lucian

Graham, Don, 96*n* 8

Grappe, Touline, 100*n* 3

Griffe, 98*n* 3

Gulf of Mexico, 11, 61, 101*n* 17, 104*n* 4

habitant/habitation, 102*n* 21

Haiti. *See* Saint-Domingue (Haiti)

hangar, 10, 16

Havana cigars, 25

head adornments, as cultural icons: planter's hat, 62; sombrero, 13, 62; veil, tortoiseshell comb, 22, 62; white muslin kerchief, 62

Henson, Margaret Swett, 101*n* 2

Herrera, Gen. Simón de, xiv, 95*n* 1

Hispanic, 61

Honour, Hugh, 14, 99*n* 6

horses: in art, 14; Pavie's background with, 15; racing, xiv, 12. *See also* fauna

Houston, Sam, 101*n* 11

Hudson Bay Co., 29, 101*n* 13

Hugo, Victor: friendship with Pavies, 3–4; influence on Théodore Pavie, 98*n* 1; slave character, xvi

Hunter, Dr. John Dunn, 101*n* 6

Iguala, Plan of, 60

Ile aux vâches plantation, 101*n* 16

Ile Brevelle, 52

India, Pavie's visit to, xviii

Indian agent, 27, 28

Indian epic (*The Mahabharata*), xvi

Jacinta, xviii, 61, 62, 63

Jackson, Andrew, 60

Jean Laffite, xviii

Jefferson, Thomas, xiii, xiv; correspondence with Madison, 95*n* 1; Louisiana Purchase, xiii, xiv, 95*n* 1

July Revolution (France: July 1830), 16, 18

Kadohadacho, xiii

Lac de la Terre noire, (Lake Sibley), 39
Laffite, Pierre & Jean, xviii, 60, 61, 104n 4
Lakmé (Delibes), xviii, 97–98n 18
Lamar, Mirabeau B., 101n 11
land grants, 21, 28
La Rabouilleuse (Balzac) 97n 14
Last of the Mohicans, The (Cooper), 14
Latin America, 104n 5
Law of April 6, 1830, xv, 11, 13, 15
lazo/lasso (lariat), xv, 10–16 passim, 96n 7, 98n 2
L'Héroïne du Texas (anonymous), 96n 7
Life of Krishna, xvi
local color, 4, 102n 21
log house (log cabin or "block house"), 103n 26
Loire Valley, xiv
London, 14
Louisiana, xi–xviii passim, 3–4, 29–30, 60–63, 96n 1, 98n 2, 99n 3, 100n 3, 101nn 16, 17, 102nn 20–24, 103n 33, 104nn 2, 9
Louis-Philippe, King of the French, 99n 5
Lower Louisiana, 102n 20

MacDonald, Archie P., 100n 1
Madison, James, xiii, 95n 1
Masons: Charles Pavie, 13; Richard Fields, 26
Matamoros, Mexico, 10
Mazeppa (Théodore Géricault), 14
Mephistopheles (Santa Anna), 10
Mercury, 4
Mexican Texas, xii–xviii passim, 10–16 passim, 26–28, 60, 61; border, xiv, 53; convoy 53; costume of traveler, 65

Mexican troops: description of uniforms, 12, 17; reinforcement of, 10
Mills, Elizabeth Shown, 100n 3
Mills, Gary B., 98n 3
Monsieur, 102n 19
music: background of Pavie, 4; banjos, 6; chants, 6; guitar, 5; mandolin 5; romanzas, 16; Spanish love song, 19; violin, 40
Mountain, the, 12
Myth of Sabine, xiii

Nacogdoches, xiii, xiv, xv, xvii, xviii, 4, 10, 11, 12, 15; description of, 16–17, 18, 26, 27, 28, 31
Nac-to-Nac, xiii, 15
Napoleonic campaigns, xiv
Natchitoches, xiii, xiv, xvii, xviii, 28, 30, 61, 62, 63; river port, 101n 17; the "village," 104n 9
Native Americans, xiv, xv, 30, 31; Cherokee, 13, 21, 26, 27, 28, 30, 95, 100n 2; Comanche, xiv, xviii, 4, 27; Delaware, 18; distribution of presents, 27–28; Hainais, xiii; Kadohadacho, xiii
nature, xvii, 12, 29
Nègre, connotations of, 98
Neutral Ground, xiv, xviii, 15, 26, 60, 62, 95n 1
New Orleans, xv, 13, 15, 60, 61, 63; the "city," 104n 9
New World, icons of, 3, 12, 13
noble savage, xv

Old Stone Fort, xiv, 27
Old World, icons of, 14
Ouachita (Washita) or Black River, 3, 102n 20

parrots (Carolina parroquets), 25, 38
Partin, James G., 98–99n 2
Pastry War. See War

Souvenirs atlantiques (cont.)
63; shift in attitude toward Piedras,
15; translation, 96n 6, 101n 12
Spain/Spanish, xiii–xiv, 3, 11, 19, 60–
61; floating borderlands, 95n 2; in-
vasion of Mexico (1829), 11
squatters, 28, 102n 23
Steddam's racetrack, 12
Streeter, Thomas W., 96n 7
Stubbs, George, 14, 99n 9
Study of the First Four Novels of Texas
(Sheehan), 96n 7
sweet gum roots, uses of, 99n 10
Swift, 11

Tejano hero, xv
Tennessee, 100n 2
Terán, Manuel de Mier y, 11
Texas, xi, xiv–xviii, 10–15 passim, 26–
28, 60–61, 95nn 1, 2, 5, 98n 2,
100nn 2, 4, 101nn 6, 11
Texas literature, xv, 96n 7
Tocqueville, Alexis de, 97n 13
trees. *See* flora

Trespalacios, Col., 100n 4

United States, xiii, 12, 15, 29, 97n 12,
99n 2
Upper Louisiana, 102n 20

Vendée region, xvi, 96–97n 11
Vera Cruz, 10, 11, 12, 15

Wales, Welsh, 60, 62
War: Mexican, xiii, xvii; Pastry, xvii, 19,
104n 1
Ward, 12
Washita, 3
Western Australia, 62
Western literature, themes of, xv
West Florida, 102n 20
West Texas, xviii
Wilkinson, Gen. James A., xiv, 95n 1
Winkler, 27, 100n 4, 101n 8
Wise, Marie Norris, 101n 16

Ybarbo, Lucian, 12
Yarborough, 12, 14